APR 2012

W9-ANC-687

3 9223 036696477

KHCPL SOUTH
1755 East Center Road
Kokomo, Indiana 46902-5393
765.453.4150
www.KHCPL.org

Kokomo-Howard County PUBLIC LIBRARY

EAR, NOSE, AND THROAT

THE HUMAN BODY

EAR, NOSE, AND THROAT

EDITED BY KARA ROGERS, SENIOR EDITOR, BIOMEDICAL SCIENCES

KOKOMO HOWARD COUNTY PUBLIC LIBRARY
KOKOMO, INDIANA
2

Britannica®
Educational Publishing

IN ASSOCIATION WITH

ROSEN
EDUCATIONAL SERVICES

Published in 2012 by Britannica Educational Publishing
(a trademark of Encyclopædia Britannica, Inc.)
in association with Rosen Educational Services, LLC
29 East 21st Street, New York, NY 10010.

Copyright © 2012 Encyclopædia Britannica, Inc. Britannica, Encyclopædia Britannica, and the Thistle logo are registered trademarks of Encyclopædia Britannica, Inc. All rights reserved.

Rosen Educational Services materials copyright © 2012 Rosen Educational Services, LLC. All rights reserved.

Distributed exclusively by Rosen Educational Services.
For a listing of additional Britannica Educational Publishing titles, call toll free (800) 237-9932.

First Edition

Britannica Educational Publishing
Michael I. Levy: Executive Editor
J.E. Luebering: Senior Manager
Marilyn L. Barton: Senior Coordinator, Production Control
Steven Bosco: Director, Editorial Technologies
Lisa S. Braucher: Senior Producer and Data Editor
Yvette Charboneau: Senior Copy Editor
Kathy Nakamura: Manager, Media Acquisition
Kara Rogers: Senior Editor, Biomedical Sciences

Rosen Educational Services
Alexandra Hanson-Harding: Editor
Nelson Sá: Art Director
Cindy Reiman: Photography Manager
Matthew Cauli: Designer, Cover Design
Introduction by Monique Vescia

Library of Congress Cataloging-in-Publication Data

Ear, nose, and throat / edited by Kara Rogers.—1st ed.
    p. cm.—(The human body)
"In association with Britannica Educational Publishing, Rosen Educational Services."
Includes bibliographical references and index.
ISBN 978-1-61530-657-2 (library binding)
1. Otolaryngology—Popular works. I. Rogers, Kara.
RF59.E17 2012
617.5'1—dc23

                                                2011013432

Manufactured in the United States of America

On the cover: A side view of the ear, nose, and throat. © *SuperStock, Inc.*

On page x: Dr. Maura Shea examines a patient's ear through an otoscope at the Codman Square Health Center April 11, 2006, in Dorchester, Massachusetts. *Joe Raedle/Getty Images*

On pages 1, 28, 60, 93, 118, 140, 165, 167, 170, 172: The human inner ear. *Shutterstock.com*

CONTENTS

Introduction   x

Chapter 1: Anatomy of the Human Ear   1

The Outer Ear   4

The Tympanic Membrane and Middle Ear   5

    Auditory Ossicles   6

    Muscles of the Middle Ear   8

    Nerves of the Middle Ear   9

    Eustachian Tube   10

The Inner Ear   11

    Vestibular System   12

    Cochlea   17

Endolymph and Perilymph   26

Chapter 2: Hearing and Balance   28

The Physiology of Hearing   28

    Transmission of Sound Waves Through the Outer and Middle Ear   30

    Transmission of Sound within the Inner Ear   36

    Cochlear Nerve and Central Auditory Pathways   44

    Analysis of Sound by the Auditory Nervous System   48

The Physiology of Balance   51

    Detection of Angular Acceleration: Dynamic Equilibrium   54

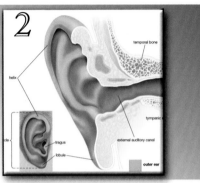

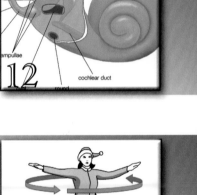

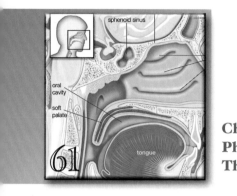

Detection of Linear
Acceleration: Static
Equilibrium   56
Disturbances of the
Vestibular System   57

**Chapter 3: Anatomy and
Physiology of the Nose and
Throat**   **60**
  Structures of the Nose and
  Nasal Cavity   60
    The Nose   61
    Nasal Concha   62
    Paranasal Air Sinuses   63
    Palate   65
  The Throat and Associated
  Structures   67
    Pharynx   67
    Larynx   69
    Vocal Cords   71
    Tonsils   72
    Adenoids   72
  The Physiology of Taste
  and Smell   75
    Taste Sense   76
    Nerve Supply   78
    Physiological Basis of Taste   79
    The Qualities of Taste   80
    Flavour   83
    Factors Affecting Taste
    Sensitivity   84
    Food Choice   86
  Smell Sense   87
    Olfactory Qualities   88
    Odourous Substances   89
    Odour Sensitivity   90
    Effects on Behaviour   91

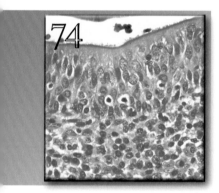

Chapter 4: Diseases of the Ear 93
  Diseases of the Outer Ear 94
    Infections and Injuries
    of the Outer Ear 95
    Deformities and Other
    Conditions of the
    Outer Ear 98
  Diseases of the Middle Ear 100
    Acute Middle-Ear
    Infection 101
    Chronic Middle-Ear
    Infection 103
    Ossicular Interruption 104
    Otosclerosis 105
  Diseases of the Inner Ear 107
    Congenital Nerve
    Deafness 108
    Viral Nerve Deafness 110
  Effects of Injury and Trauma 110
    Ototoxic Drugs 111
    Skull Fracture and
    Concussion 111
    Exposure to Noise 111
  Inflammation and Tumours 113
    Acoustic Neuroma 113
    Labyrinthitis 113
    Ménière Disease 114
    Presbycusis 114
    Tinnitus 115

**Chapter 5: Communication
Disorders Involving
Structures of the Ear, Nose,
and Throat** 118
  Prevalence of Communication
  Disorders 118
  Speech Disorders 119

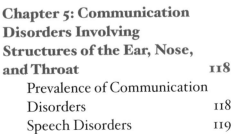

Voice Disorders   121
Articulation Disorders   123
   Cluttering   123
   Lisping   124
   Stuttering, or Stammering   124
Speech of the Hard of
Hearing   127
Speech Impediments from
Defective Articulators   129
   Tongue-Tie   129
   Loss of Tongue   130
   Nasal Speech   130
   Cleft Palate Speech   132
Treatment and Rehabilitation   135
Development of Speech
Correction   136
   Speech Synthesis   138
   Pseudolaryngeal Speech   139

Chapter 6: Disorders of the Nose and Throat and Approaches to Ear, Nose, and Throat Evaluation

Chapter 6: Disorders of the
Nose and Throat and
Approaches to Ear, Nose,
and Throat Evaluation   140
Notable Diseases and Disorders
of the nose and Throat   140
   Laryngeal Cancer   141
   Nasal Polyp   142
   Nosebleed   142
   Oral and Oropharyngeal
   Cancer   144
   Sinus Disorders   147
Approaches to Ear, Nose, and
Throat Evaluation   148
   Otolaryngology   148
   Nasopharyn-
   golaryngoscopy   149

Hearing Tests and
    Rehabilitation   149
Conclusion   165

Glossary   167
Bibliography   170
Index   172

INTRODUCTION

When an airplane begins its initial descent, passengers often chew gum or yawn to clear their ears because they feel bothered by changes in air pressure. The common cold is notorious for obscuring our ability to taste food. Common experiences such as these demonstrate the close physiological relationships shared by the ear, nose, and throat. These tissues, however, also perform separate functions within the human body. As you'll discover in this book, the ear, nose, and throat play key roles in the respiratory and alimentary systems and are essential to the body's health. At the same time, each of these tissues performs a unique function. For example, the structures of the throat enable vocal expression, the ear enables hearing and balance, and the nose is central to the senses of taste and smell. Until the late 19th century, however, physicians considered each organ separately. For example, otologists specialized exclusively in the ear, and laryngologists diagnosed and treated disorders of the throat and larynx. Once the interdependence of the ear, the nose, and the throat came to be better understood, the medical sciences of otology and laryngology were unified in a specialized field—otolaryngology—devoted to the study and treatment of diseases and disorders associated with all three organs. Today, otolaryngology is often referred to simply as "ENT" (short for ear, nose, and throat).

When scientists began studying the design of the human ear, they often used architectural terms to describe its features. Hence, the human ear is said to have walls and windows, a vestibule, and a ceiling. In William Shakespeare's play *Hamlet*, one character kills another by pouring poison into "the porches of his ears." The inner ear even includes two labyrinths, one inside the other. This highly developed organ is responsible for two entirely different functions: the sense of hearing and the sense of equilibrium. The latter is governed by the vestibular system and enables an individual to maintain his or her balance. For hearing, the ear transforms the vibrations of sound waves into nerve impulses, which the brain then interprets as sound. Scientists do not fully understand the extremely complex process by which vibrations in mediums such as air and water are ultimately recognized by the brain as sound. They do know, however, that in the ear the energy of sound experiences a unique transformation from wave vibration to nerve impulse. This impulse is responsible for relaying information about sound waves to the sound-processing centre of the brain.

The process of hearing begins in the outer ear, where vibrations in the air are channeled toward the tympanic membrane, or eardrum, in the middle ear. There, the vibrations are transferred to the eardrum and to minute ear bones known as ossicles. These movements create vibrations in the fluid of the cochlea, a structure in the inner ear that contains the sensory organ of hearing and that is distinguished by its coiled shape, which resembles a snail's shell. The vibrations in the cochlear fluid create waves that travel along the basilar membrane (one of three membranes in the cochlea). These waves then stimulate hair cells in a structure known as the organ of Corti. The hair cells convert the waves to nerve impulses, which are then transmitted to the brainstem for processing.

The ear bones found in the middle ear are present in the ears of all mammals. These bones consist of the malleus, the incus, and the stapes, which are commonly referred to as the hammer, the anvil, and the stirrup, respectively. The ear contains the smallest bones in the human body, and hearing would be impossible without them.

Various devices and methods for evaluating hearing have been developed over the years, including the audiometer, the electrocochleogram (ECoG), and brainstem-evoked response audiometry (BERA). Audiologists also rely on a far simpler diagnostic tool: the tuning fork.

In addition to hearing, the ear is also responsible for equilibrium, the body's specific sense of orientation with respect to gravity. As is often the case in the history of science, researchers have learned much about an organism by observing the effects of a specific injury. Hair cells in the vestibule and semicircular canals of the inner ear are critical to postural equilibrium, and when these structures are damaged or destroyed, an individual will suffer from vertigo (a false sense of turning or falling) and disorientation.

Each part of the ear is vulnerable to specific diseases and disorders. The outer ear can be subject to frostbite, and in boxers repeated blows to the sides of the head can give rise to "cauliflower ear," a type of cartilage injury in the outer ear. Foreign substances may enter the tissues of the outer ear and cause problems such as perichondritis, which is an inflammation of the outer ear that comes from swimming in contaminated water. The proximity of the middle ear cavity to the brain causes potential dangers if an ear infection is left untreated. Many of these conditions can be alleviated with antibiotics. Ironically, antibiotics such as streptomycin can also be ototoxic, or harmful to the ear. Disorders of the inner ear, such as Ménière disease, may affect the sufferer's hearing or equilibrium or both. The rubella virus contracted by women during the first term of pregnancy caused congenital nerve deafness in many babies until 1969, when a vaccine was developed. With age, many people experience gradual hearing loss as a result of presbycusis, and 10–15 percent of the population suffers from chronic tinnitus, a persistent ringing or buzzing in the ears. The hair cells in the ear, a vital part of the mechanics of hearing, do not repair themselves after they are damaged as do other tissues in the human body. If scientists can find a way to help these hair cells regenerate, there may one day be a cure for profound hearing loss.

Since speech acquisition is dependent upon hearing, loss of hearing in young children resulting from injury or disease can hamper or arrest speech development. Audiologists measure degrees of hearing impairment, and otologists use surgery or medicine to treat diseases and defects of the ear. Many people with severe hearing loss depend on hearing aids, which must be fine-tuned for each individual's needs. Those who experience hearing loss can also benefit from learning lip reading and American Sign Language (ASL) in order to communicate with other signers. A more recent advance in technology is the cochlear implant, a device that works by stimulating the nerve fibres in the inner ear. Cochlear implants have generated controversy within the deaf community, where many object to the characterization of deafness as a disorder that needs to be cured.

References to the nose also make use of architectural terms. For example, the nose has a floor, a roof, walls, and even a vestibule. The nose and the mouth share the hard palate, which is formed in part by the palatine bone. A flap of tissue called the soft palate extends back to the nasopharynx, or nasal portion of the throat, and prevents chewed food and fluids from going up into the nose while eating. The facial bones around the nose contain hollow spaces, the site of the paranasal sinuses, which reduce the weight of the skull and add resonance to the voice.

The nose conditions inhaled air before it enters the lungs. In addition to serving as the entrance to the respiratory tract, the nose is also the source of the olfactory organ and hence is the site of smell. Odorants in the air stimulate the chemoreceptors in the nose, which transmit electrical impulses to the brain, where they are interpreted as specific odours. Saying that we smell with our noses has been likened to claiming that we hear with our earlobes—the most visible portion of the organ has little to do with the actual process of detecting smells.

While humans may not have the highly tuned sense of smell on which dogs and other animals depend, our olfactory sense is still far more refined and acute than our sense of taste. The average person can detect up to 10,000 different odours. Smell functions like an early warning system, letting us know when food has spoiled or when the gas on the stove has failed to ignite. The olfactory bulb that helps convert sensory stimulation into perception is part of the limbic system, the brain's emotional centre. Early in life, very personal connections are made in our brains between certain odours and experiences, and a smell can immediately trigger a very specific memory. Catch a whiff of cinnamon, and suddenly you're a child again, standing in your grandmother's warm kitchen. Smells can alter mood and affect how well someone performs on the job. The fascinating relationship between the human olfactory sense and emotion has intrigued writers as well as neuroscientists. Perfumers, real estate agents, and advertisers have all found ways to capitalize on this connection.

One procedure for examining the nose, sinuses, and throat is called nasopharyngolaryngoscopy. Conditions specific to the nose include nasal polyps (usually the result of allergies), nosebleeds, and disorders such as sinusitis, an inflammation of the mucosal lining of the paranasal sinuses. The inability to perceive smell is called anosmia. People who suffer from this condition, which may be brought on by a head injury or sinus disease, also have very little sense of taste, because of the relationship between these senses.

The human throat, or pharynx, connects the back of the mouth and the nose to the esophagus and the trachea, or windpipe. This muscular passageway ensures that food is carried to the stomach and that air travels to the lungs. The larynx, or voice box, at the top of the trachea is another organ that serves a dual function within the body. This tubular structure channels air to the lungs and is the site of the vocal cords, which produce vocal sounds.

Individuals such as singers and announcers, who use their voices often, may develop small tumours on the larynx. These small growths, known as papillomas, generally are benign. Patients who have had their larynx removed, typically because of a severe disease such as laryngeal cancer, can learn to communicate with the aid of an electronic speech synthesizer. They can also be taught esophageal speech, a practice that involves swallowing air into the esophagus and belching it out in a controlled manner to produce recognizable speech sounds.

The tonsils are oval-shaped masses situated in the throat on either side of the pharynx. They are believed to aid in the production of antibodies that help prevent infection. However, the tonsils may themselves become infected, a condition called tonsillitis. Surgical removal of the tonsils, or tonsillectomy, is an ancient procedure that is still one of the most common surgeries performed on children in the United States. In 1906 the Tonsillectomy Riots were sparked when 50,000 immigrant mothers descended on public schools in New York City in protest of the tonsillectomies being performed on their children. While doctors still routinely remove tonsils in children, people continue to question the necessity of the procedure.

Communication disorders have always plagued people, judging from Biblical references to problems with speech. Such disorders may stem from physical or psychological causes or a combination of these factors. Communication disorders occur disproportionally in human populations: There are far more cases of cleft palate among Native

American than African American children, for instance, and far more men stutter than women. Preferred methods for treating speech afflictions also differ from one country or culture to another.

The word language has its roots in the Latin lingua, meaning "tongue." In addition to enabling us to articulate sounds, the tongue helps us to chew and swallow our food and to taste what we are ingesting, yet another example of the body's remarkable economy. Taste buds on the tongue's surface contain receptors that transmit five different sensations of flavour—sweet, sour, salty, bitter, and umami (a Japanese term roughly translated as "savouriness")—to the nervous system. What we identify as the flavour of food is a combination of taste, touch, smell, texture or consistency, and sensations of temperature. Just as with smell, individuals' responses to tastes differ widely due to both cultural and personal preferences. Most people have heard of colour blindness, but there is such a thing as taste blindness too, in which certain individuals are unable to detect the bitter flavour of particular chemicals.

Each day people go about their business, performing highly complex actions without a second thought: chewing and swallowing a snack, recognizing a friend's voice on the phone, or noticing the scent of clean sheets on the bed. Thanks to the ear, nose, and throat and how effectively they function together within our bodies, we take most of these actions for granted. Yet researchers still marvel at the design of these remarkable organs and admit that they do not fully understand how the senses of smell, taste, and hearing work. Thus, many mysteries of these organs and their functions are still waiting to be solved.

CHAPTER 1

ANATOMY OF THE HUMAN EAR

The senses of hearing, smell, and taste, and the human ability to speak and produce sound, facilitate human survival and undeniably enrich the human experience. The intricate structure of the ear, with its outer parts designed to funnel sound waves into the inner ear, where they are converted into electrical impulses that travel to the auditory nucleus (or sound-processing region) of the brain, enhances our survival by allowing us to detect sounds associated with potential danger. The ability to perceive pitch and distinguish between musical tones is arguably among the most affective features of hearing, enabling us to derive enjoyment from music and song. The human production of sound, in the form of speech and song, is made possible by the larynx (or voice box) and vocal cords and is influenced by surrounding structures of the throat and oral and nasal cavities.

The senses of smell and taste likewise enrich our lives. The sense of smell, or olfaction, is housed in a special membrane layer in the nose, which is lined with unique receptor cells that trap odour molecules and communicate information about these molecules to the brain, where the information is interpreted and perceived as smell. Taste, or gustation, which is imparted by special taste receptor cells clustered into taste buds on the tongue, combines with smell to produce the attribute of flavour. The human perception of flavour is a major factor in our enjoyment of food and greatly influences the culinary arts.

Although the ear, nose, and throat are structurally diverse, they are united by the fact that they serve important roles in both human survival and cultural experience. In addition, despite their individual uniqueness of form, they are associated anatomically. For example, the throat and ear communicate with one another via the eustachian tubes, and the nose and throat are connected by passages that facilitate the drainage of mucus from the sinuses (cavities) of the head. Hence, each component is influenced by the other. This is most evident in diseases and disorders that affect the tissues of these structures.

The exploration of the ear, nose, and throat in this volume begins with the human ear. In addition to hearing, the ear serves a fundamental role in maintaining a sense of balance. Thus, it detects and analyzes noises by transduction (or the conversion of sound waves into

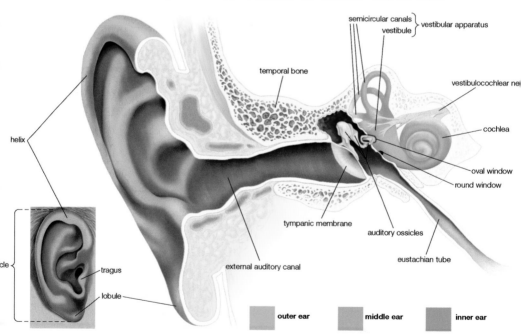

The structures of the outer, middle, and inner ear. Encyclopædia Britannica, Inc.

electrochemical impulses), and it influences postural equilibrium, or balance, and coordinates movements of the head and eyes.

Anatomically the ear has three distinguishable parts: the outer, middle, and inner ear. The outer ear consists of the visible portion called the auricle, or pinna, which projects from the side of the head, and the short external auditory canal, the inner end of which is closed by the tympanic membrane, commonly called the eardrum. The function of the outer ear is to collect sound waves and guide them to the tympanic membrane. The middle ear is a narrow, air-filled cavity in the temporal bone. It is spanned by a chain of three tiny bones—the malleus (hammer), incus (anvil), and stapes (stirrup), collectively called the auditory ossicles. This ossicular chain conducts sound from the tympanic membrane to the inner ear, which has been known since the time of Galen, a prominent physician in the 2nd century CE, as the labyrinth. It is a complicated system of fluid-filled passages and cavities located deep within the petrous portion of the temporal bone. The temporal bone is the bone that contains the internal auditory organs, and the petrous part of the temporal bone is an especially dense and hard part of that bone. The inner ear consists of two functional units: the vestibular apparatus and the snail-shell-like cochlea. The vestibular apparatus consists of the vestibule and semicircular canals, which contains the sensory organs of postural equilibrium, and the cochlea contains the sensory organ of hearing. Both sensory organs are highly specialized endings of the eighth cranial nerve, also called the vestibulocochlear nerve. The cranial nerves are a group of 12 pairs of nerves that connect the brainstem and other parts of the brain to the sense organs of the head as well as to muscles, internal organs, and glands in the head, neck, chest, and upper abdomen.

THE OUTER EAR

The most striking differences between the human ear and the ears of other mammals are in the structure of the outermost part, the auricle. In humans the auricle is an almost rudimentary, usually immobile shell that lies close to the side of the head. It consists of a thin plate of yellow fibrocartilage covered by closely adherent skin. The cartilage is molded into clearly defined hollows, ridges, and furrows that form an irregular, shallow funnel. The deepest depression, which leads directly to the external auditory canal, or acoustic meatus, is called the concha. It is partly covered by two small projections, the tongue-like tragus in front and the antitragus behind. Above the tragus a prominent ridge, the helix, arises from the floor of the concha and continues as the incurved rim of the upper portion of the auricle. An inner, concentric ridge, the antihelix, surrounds the concha and is separated from the helix by a furrow, the scapha, also called the fossa of the helix.

In some ears a little prominence known as Darwin's tubercle is seen along the upper, posterior portion of the helix. It is the vestige of the folded-over point of the ear of a remote human ancestor. The lobule, the fleshy lower part of the auricle, is the only area of the outer ear that contains no cartilage. The auricle also has several small rudimentary muscles, which fasten it to the skull and scalp. In most individuals these muscles do not function, although some persons can voluntarily activate them to produce limited movements. The external auditory canal is a slightly curved tube that extends inward from the floor of the concha and ends blindly at the tympanic membrane. In its outer third the wall of the canal consists of cartilage, and in its inner two-thirds, of bone. The entire length of the passage (24 mm, or almost 1 inch) is lined with skin, which also covers the outer surface of the tympanic membrane. Fine hairs directed outward and modified sweat glands that produce earwax, or cerumen, line the canal and discourage insects from entering it.

THE TYMPANIC MEMBRANE AND MIDDLE EAR

The thin, semitransparent tympanic membrane, or eardrum, which forms the boundary between the outer and middle ear, is stretched obliquely across the end of the external canal. Its diameter is about 9 mm (0.35 inch), its shape that of a flattened cone with its apex directed inward. Thus, its outer surface is slightly concave. The edge of the membrane is thickened and attached to a groove in an incomplete ring of bone, the tympanic annulus, which almost encircles it and holds it in place. The uppermost small area of the membrane where the ring is open is slack and is called the pars flaccida, but the far greater portion is tightly stretched and is called the pars tensa. The appearance and mobility of the tympanic membrane are important for the diagnosis of middle-ear disease, which is especially common in young children. When viewed with a medical instrument called an otoscope, the healthy membrane is translucent and pearl-gray in colour, sometimes with a pinkish or yellowish tinge.

The entire tympanic membrane consists of three layers. The outer layer of skin is continuous with that of the external canal. The inner layer of mucous membrane is continuous with the lining of the tympanic cavity of the middle ear. Between these layers is a layer of fibrous tissue made up of circular and radial fibres that give the membrane its stiffness and tension. The membrane is well supplied with blood vessels and sensory nerve fibres that make it acutely sensitive to pain.

The cavity of the middle ear is a narrow, air-filled space. A slight constriction divides it into an upper and a lower chamber, the tympanum (tympanic cavity) proper below and the epitympanum above. These chambers also are referred to as the atrium and attic, respectively. The middle-ear space roughly resembles a rectangular room with four walls, a floor, and a ceiling. The outer (lateral) wall of the middle-ear space is formed by the tympanic membrane. Its ceiling (superior wall) is a thin plate of bone that separates it from the cranial cavity and brain above. The floor (inferior wall) is also a thin bony plate separating the cavity from the jugular vein and carotid artery below. The back (posterior) wall partly separates it from another cavity, the mastoid antrum, but an opening in this wall leads to the antrum and to the small air cells of the mastoid process (a process is a projecting part of an organic structure), which is the roughened, slightly bulging portion of the temporal bone just behind the external auditory canal and the auricle. In the front (anterior) wall is the opening of the eustachian, or auditory, tube, which connects the middle ear with the nasopharynx, a tubular passageway from the back of the nose into the throat. The inner (medial) wall, which separates the middle ear from the inner ear, or labyrinth, is a part of the otic capsule, a bony structure that surrounds the inner ear. The inner wall has two small openings, or fenestrae, one above the other. The upper one is the oval window, which is closed by the footplate of the stapes. The lower one is the round window, which is covered by a thin membrane.

AUDITORY OSSICLES

Crossing the middle-ear cavity is the short ossicular chain formed by three tiny bones that link the tympanic membrane with the oval window and inner ear. From the

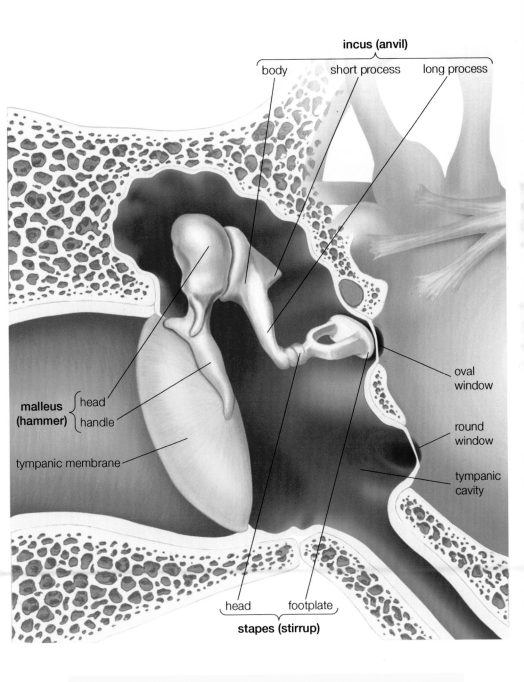

The auditory ossicles of the middle ear and the structures surrounding them.
Encyclopædia Britannica, Inc.

outside inward they are the malleus (hammer), the incus (anvil), and the stapes (stirrup). The malleus more closely resembles a club than a hammer, and the incus looks more like a premolar tooth with uneven roots than an anvil. These bones are suspended by ligaments, which leave the chain free to vibrate in transmitting sound from the tympanic membrane to the inner ear.

The malleus consists of a handle and a head. The handle is firmly attached to the tympanic membrane from the centre (umbo) to the upper margin. The head of the malleus and the body of the incus are joined tightly and are suspended in the epitympanum just above the upper rim of the tympanic annulus, where three small ligaments anchor the head of the malleus to the walls and roof of the epitympanum. Another minute ligament fixes the short process (crus) of the incus in a shallow depression, called the fossa incudis, in the rear wall of the cavity. The long process of the incus is bent near its end and bears a small bony knob that forms a loose, ligament-enclosed joint with the head of the stapes. The stapes is the smallest bone in the body. It is about 3 mm (0.1 inch) long and weighs scarcely 3 mg (0.0001 ounce). It lies almost horizontally, at right angles to the process of the incus. Its base, or footplate, fits nicely in the oval window and is surrounded by the elastic annular ligament, although it remains free to vibrate in transmitting sound to the labyrinth.

MUSCLES OF THE MIDDLE EAR

Two minuscule muscles are located in the middle ear. The longer muscle, called the tensor tympani, emerges from a bony canal just above the opening of the eustachian tube and runs backward then outward as it changes direction in passing over a pulleylike projection of bone. The tendon of this muscle is attached to the upper part of the handle of the malleus. When contracted, the tensor tympani tends to pull the malleus inward and thus maintains or increases the tension of the tympanic membrane. The shorter, stouter muscle, called the stapedius, arises from the back wall of the middle-ear cavity and extends forward and attaches to the neck of the head of the stapes. Its reflex contractions tend to tip the stapes backward, as if to pull it out of the oval window. Thus it selectively reduces the intensity of sounds entering the inner ear, especially those of lower frequency.

NERVES OF THE MIDDLE EAR

As was mentioned earlier, there are 12 sets of cranial nerves. They include sensory nerves, motor nerves, and mixed nerves. The cranial nerves connected to the sense organs relay information about smell, vision, hearing, and taste to the brain. Cranial nerves also control the muscles involved in making facial expressions, chewing, swallowing, and moving the eyes, head, shoulders, and neck. One of the more complex in function is the seventh cranial nerve, called the facial nerve. It passes by a somewhat circuitous route through the facial canal in the petrous portion of the temporal bone on its way from the brainstem to the muscles of expression of the face. A small but important branch, the chorda tympani nerve, emerges from the canal in the middle ear cavity and runs forward along the inner surface of the pars tensa of the membrane, passing between the handle of the malleus and the long process of the incus. Since at this point it is covered only by the tympanic mucous membrane, it appears to be quite bare. Then it resumes its course through the

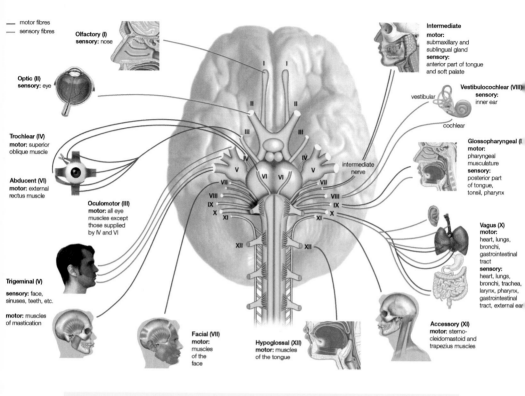

motor fibres
sensory fibres

Olfactory (I)
sensory: nose

Optic (II)
sensory: eye

Trochlear (IV)
motor: superior
oblique muscle

Abducent (VI)
motor: external
rectus muscle

Oculomotor (III)
motor: all eye
muscles except
those supplied
by IV and VI

Trigeminal (V)
sensory: face,
sinuses, teeth, etc.
motor: muscles
of mastication

Facial (VII)
motor:
muscles
of the
face

Hypoglossal (XII)
motor: muscles
of the tongue

Intermediate
motor:
submaxillary and
sublingual gland
sensory:
anterior part of tongue
and soft palate

Vestibulocochlear (VIII)
vestibular
sensory:
inner ear
cochlear

Glossopharyngeal (IX)
motor:
pharyngeal
musculature
sensory:
posterior part
of tongue,
tonsil, pharynx

intermediate
nerve

Vagus (X)
motor:
heart, lungs,
bronchi,
gastrointestinal
tract
sensory:
heart, lungs,
bronchi, trachea,
larynx, pharynx,
gastrointestinal
tract, external ear

Accessory (XI)
motor: sterno-
cleidomastoid and
trapezius muscles

There are 12 pairs of cranial nerves that function to control the muscles and sense organs of the head and thoracic region. Encyclopædia Britannica, Inc.

anterior bony wall, bringing sensory fibres for taste to the anterior two-thirds of the tongue and parasympathetic secretory fibres to salivary glands.

EUSTACHIAN TUBE

The eustachian tube, about 45 mm (1.75 inches) long, leads downward and inward from the tympanum to the naso-pharynx, the space that is behind and continuous with the nasal passages and is above the soft palate. At its upper end the tube is narrow and surrounded by bone. Nearer the pharynx it widens and becomes cartilaginous. Its mucous lining, which is continuous with that of the middle ear, is covered with cilia, small hairlike projections whose coordinated rhythmical sweeping motions speed the drainage of mucous secretions from the tympanum to the pharynx.

The eustachian tube helps to ventilate the middle ear and to maintain equal air pressure on both sides of the tympanic membrane. The tube is closed at rest and opens during swallowing so that minor pressure differences are adjusted without conscious effort. During a dive or a rapid descent in an airplane the tube may remain tightly closed. The discomfort that is felt as the external pressure increases can usually be overcome by attempting a forced expiration with the mouth and nostrils held tightly shut. This maneuver, which raises the air pressure in the pharynx and causes the tube to open, is called Valsalva's maneuver and is named for Italian physician-anatomist Antonio Maria Valsalva (1666–1723), who recommended it for clearing pus from an infected middle ear.

THE INNER EAR

There are actually two labyrinths of the inner ear, one inside the other—the membranous labyrinth contained within the bony labyrinth. The bony labyrinth consists of a central chamber called the vestibule, the three semicircular canals, and the spirally coiled cochlea. Within each structure, and filling only a fraction of the available space, is a corresponding portion of the membranous labyrinth: the vestibule contains the utricle and saccule, each semicircular canal its semicircular duct, and the cochlea its cochlear duct. Surrounding the membranous labyrinth and filling the remaining space is the watery fluid called perilymph. It is derived from blood plasma and resembles but is not identical to the cerebrospinal fluid of the brain.

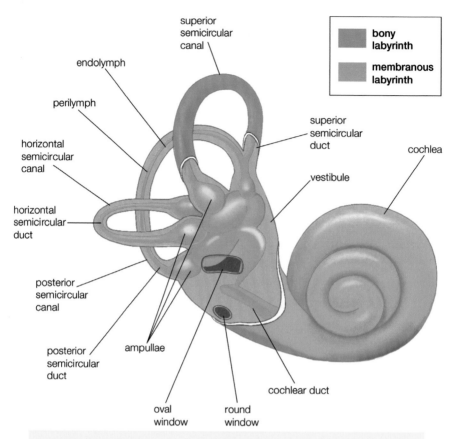

The two labyrinths of the inner ear. The bony labyrinth is partially cut away to show the membranous labyrinth within. Encyclopædia Britannica, Inc.

Like most of the hollow organs, the membranous labyrinth is lined with epithelium (a sheet of specialized cells that covers internal and external body surfaces). It is filled with a different fluid, called endolymph. Because the membranous labyrinth is a closed system, the endolymph and perilymph do not mix.

VESTIBULAR SYSTEM

The vestibular system is the apparatus of the inner ear involved in balance. It consists of two structures of the bony labyrinth, the vestibule and the semicircular canals, and the structures of the membranous labyrinth contained within them.

Vestibule

Two of the most important organs for helping humans orient their body in space are the saccule and utricle. These two tiny sacs, located in the vestibule, are known as the otolith organs. The saccule is sensitive to up and down movements of the head, and the utricle is sensitive to sideways movements. They are part of the membranous labyrinth of the inner ear into which the semicircular canals open. Because they respond to gravitational forces, they are also called gravity receptors. Each sac has on its inner surface a single patch of sensory cells called a

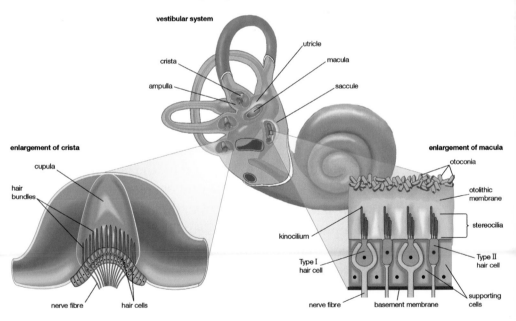

The membranous labyrinth of the vestibular system (centre), *which contains the organs of balance, and* (lower left) *the cristae of the semicircular ducts and* (lower right) *the maculae of the utricle and saccule.* Encyclopædia Britannica, Inc.

macula, which is about 2 mm (0.08 inch) in diameter and which monitors the position of the head relative to the vertical. In the utricle the macula projects from the anterior (front) wall of that tubular sac and lies primarily in the horizontal plane. In the saccule the macula is in the vertical plane and directly overlies the bone of the inner wall of the vestibule. In shape it is elongated and resembles the letter J. Each macula consists of neuroepithelium, a layer that is made up of supporting cells and sensory cells, as well as a basement membrane, nerve fibres and nerve endings, and underlying connective tissue. The sensory cells are called hair cells because of the hairlike cilia—stiff stereocilia and flexible, longer, moveable kinocilia—that project from their apexes' ends. The nerve fibres are from the superior, or vestibular, division of the vestibulocochlear nerve. They pierce the basement membrane and, depending on the type of hair cell, either end on the base of the cell or form a calyx, or cuplike structure, that surrounds it.

Each of the hair cells of the vestibular organs is topped by a hair bundle, which consists of about 100 fine, nonmotile, or nonmoveable, stereocilia of graded lengths and a single motile kinocilium. The stereocilia are anchored in a dense cuticular plate at the cell's apex. The single kinocilium, which is larger and longer than the stereocilia, rises from a noncuticular area of the cell membrane at one side of the cuticular plate. The tallest stereocilia are those closest to the kinocilium, and they decrease in length in stepwise fashion away from the kinocilium. Minute strands of filaments link the tips and shafts of neighbouring stereocilia to each other. When the hair bundles are deflected—e.g., because of a tilt of the head—the hair cells are stimulated to alter the rate of the nerve impulses that they are constantly sending via the vestibular nerve fibres to the brainstem. Covering the entire macula is the delicate otolithic, or statolithic, membrane. This membrane is sometimes described as gelatinous, although it has a fibre-like pattern. The surface of the membrane is covered by a blanket of a special type of crystals known as rhombohedral crystals. These crystals are referred to as otoconia, or statoconia, and consist of calcium carbonate in the form of calcite. The crystalline particles, which range in length from 1 to 20 micrometres (μm; there are about 25,000 μm in an inch), are much denser than the membrane—their specific gravity is almost three times that of the membrane and the endolymph—and thus add considerable mass to it.

The vestibular hair cells are of two types. Type I cells have a rounded body enclosed by a nerve calyx. Type II cells have a cylindrical body with nerve endings at the base. They form a mosaic on the surface of the maculae, with the type I cells dominating in a curvilinear area (the striola) near the centre of the macula and the cylindrical cells around the periphery. The significance of these patterns is poorly understood, but they may increase sensitivity to slight tiltings of the head.

Semicircular Canals

The three semicircular canals of the bony labyrinth are designated, according to their position, superior, horizontal, and posterior. The superior and posterior canals are in diagonal vertical planes that intersect at right angles. Each canal has an expanded end, the ampulla, which opens into the vestibule. The ampullae of the horizontal and superior canals lie close together, just above the oval window, but the ampulla of the posterior canal opens on the opposite side of the vestibule. The other ends of the superior and posterior canals join to form a common stem, or crus, which also opens into the vestibule. Nearby is the mouth of a canal called the vestibular aqueduct, which opens into the cranial cavity. The other end of the horizontal canal has a separate opening into the vestibule. Thus, the vestibule completes the circle for each of the semicircular canals.

Each of the three bony canals and their ampullae encloses a membranous semicircular duct of much smaller diameter that has its own ampulla. The membranous ducts and ampullae follow the same pattern as the canals and ampullae of the bony labyrinth, with their openings into the utricle and with a common crus for the superior and posterior ducts. Like the other parts of the membranous labyrinth, they are filled with endolymph and surrounded by perilymph. The narrow endolymphatic duct passes from the utricle through the vestibular aqueduct into the cranial cavity, carrying excess endolymph to be absorbed by the endolymphatic sac.

Each membranous ampulla contains a saddle-shaped ridge of tissue called the crista, the sensory end organ that extends across it from side to side. It is covered by neuroepithelium, with hair cells and supporting cells. From this ridge rises a gelatinous structure, the cupula, which extends to the roof of the ampulla immediately above it, dividing the interior of the ampulla into two approximately equal parts. Like the hair cells of the maculae, the hair cells of the cristae have hair bundles projecting from their apices. The kinocilium and the longest stereocilia extend far up into the substance of the cupula, occupying fine parallel channels. Thus, the cupula is attached at its base to the crista but is free to incline toward or away from the utricle in response to the slightest flow of endolymph or a change in pressure. The tufts of cilia move with the cupula and, depending on the direction of their bending, cause an increase or decrease in the rate of nerve impulse discharges carried by the vestibular nerve fibres to the brainstem.

COCHLEA

The cochlea contains the sensory organ of hearing. It bears a striking resemblance to the shell of a snail and in fact takes its name from the Greek word for this object.

Structure of the Cochlea

The cochlea is a spiral tube that is coiled two and one-half turns around a hollow central pillar, the modiolus. It forms a cone approximately 9 mm (0.35 inch) in diameter at its base and 5 mm in height. When stretched out, the tube is approximately 30 mm in length. It is widest—2 mm—at the point where the basal coil opens into the vestibule and tapers until it ends blindly at the apex. The otherwise hollow centre of the modiolus contains the cochlear artery and vein, as well as the twisted trunk of fibres of the cochlear nerve. This nerve, a division of the very short vestibulocochlear nerve, enters the base of the modiolus from the brainstem through an opening in the petrous portion of the temporal bone called the internal meatus. The spiral ganglion cells—a dense group of nerve cells—of the cochlear nerve are found in a bony spiral canal winding around the central core.

A thin bony shelf, the osseous spiral lamina, winds around the modiolus like the thread of a screw. It projects about halfway across the cochlear canal, partly dividing it into two compartments, an upper chamber called the scala vestibuli (vestibular ramp) and a lower chamber called the scala tympani (tympanic ramp). The scala vestibuli and scala tympani, which are filled with perilymph, communicate with each other through an opening at the apex of the cochlea, called the helicotrema, which can be seen if the cochlea is sliced longitudinally down the middle. At its basal end, near the middle ear, the scala vestibuli opens into the vestibule.

The basal end of the scala tympani ends blindly just below the round window. Nearby is the opening of the narrow cochlear aqueduct, through which passes the perilymphatic duct. This duct connects the interior of the cochlea with the subdural space (situated beneath the dura matter of the brain) in the posterior cranial fossa (the rear portion of the floor of the cranial cavity).

A smaller scala, called the cochlear duct (scala media), lies between the larger vestibular and tympanic scalae. It is the cochlear portion of the membranous labyrinth. Filled with endolymph, the cochlear duct ends blindly at both ends—i.e., below the round window and at the apex. In cross section this duct resembles a right triangle. Its base is formed by the osseous spiral lamina and the basilar membrane, which separate the cochlear duct from the scala tympani. Resting on the basilar membrane is the organ of Corti, which contains the hair cells that give rise to nerve signals in response to sound vibrations. The side of the triangle is formed by two tissues that line the bony wall of the cochlea, the stria vascularis, which lines the outer wall of the cochlear duct, and the fibrous spiral ligament, which lies between the stria and the bony wall of the cochlea. A layer of flat cells bounds the stria and separates it from the spiral ligament. The hypotenuse is formed by the transparent vestibular membrane of Reissner, which consists of only two layers of flattened cells. A low ridge, the spiral limbus, rests on the margin of the osseous spiral lamina. Reissner's membrane stretches from the inner margin of the limbus to the upper border of the stria.

The spiral ligament extends above the attachment of Reissner's membrane and is in contact with the perilymph in the scala vestibuli. Extending below the insertion of the basilar membrane, it is in contact with the perilymph of the scala tympani. It contains many stout fibres that anchor the basilar membrane and numerous

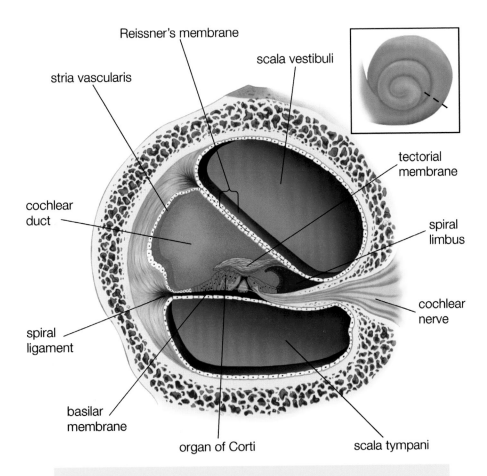

Reissner's membrane

scala vestibuli

stria vascularis

tectorial membrane

cochlear duct

spiral limbus

cochlear nerve

spiral ligament

basilar membrane

organ of Corti

scala tympani

A cross section through one of the turns of the cochlea (inset) showing the scala tympani and scala vestibuli, which contain perilymph, and the cochlear duct, which is filled with endolymph. Encyclopædia Britannica, Inc.

connective-tissue cells. Behind the stria the structure of the spiral ligament is denser than near the upper and lower margins. The spiral ligament, like the adjacent stria, is well supplied with blood vessels. It receives the radiating arterioles that pass outward from the modiolus in bony channels of the roof of the scala vestibuli. Branches from these vessels form a network of capillaries above the junction with Reissner's membrane that may be largely responsible for the formation of the perilymph from the blood plasma. Other branches enter the stria, while still others pass behind it to the spiral prominence. From these separate capillary networks, which are not interconnected, small veins descending below the attachment of the basilar membrane collect blood and deliver it to the spiral vein in the floor of the scala tympani.

At the lower margin of the stria is the spiral prominence, a low ridge parallel to the basilar membrane that contains its own set of longitudinally directed capillary vessels. Below the prominence is a furrow called the outer sulcus. The floor of the outer sulcus is lined by cells of epithelial origin, some of which send long projections into the substance of the spiral ligament. Between these so-called root cells, capillary vessels descend from the spiral ligament. This region appears to have an absorptive rather than a secretory function, and it may be involved in removing waste materials from the endolymph.

In humans the basilar membrane is about 30 to 35 mm in length. It widens from less than 0.001 mm near its basal end to 0.005 mm near the apex. The basilar membrane is spanned by stiff, elastic fibres that are connected at their basal ends in the modiolus. Their distal ends (away from the main part of the body) are embedded in the membrane but are not actually attached, which allows them to vibrate. The fibres decrease in calibre and increase in length from the basal end of the cochlea near the middle ear to the apex, so that the basilar membrane as a whole decreases remarkably in stiffness from base to apex. Furthermore, at the basal end the osseous spiral lamina is broader, the stria vascularis wider, and the spiral ligament stouter than at the apex. In contrast, however, the mass of the organ of Corti is least at the base and greatest at the apex. Thus, a certain degree of tuning is provided in the structure of the cochlear duct and its contents. With greater stiffness and less mass, the basal end is more attuned to the sounds of higher frequencies. Decreased stiffness and increased mass render the apical end more responsive to lower frequencies.

Beneath the fibrillar layer of the basilar membrane is the acellular ground substance of the membrane. This layer is covered in turn by a single layer of spindle-shaped cells called mesothelial cells, which have long processes arranged longitudinally and parallel, facing the scala tympani and forming a layer of connective tissue called the tympanic lamella that is in contact with the perilymph.

Capillary blood vessels are found on the underside of the tympanic lip of the limbus and, in some species, including the guinea pig and humans, within the basilar membrane, beneath the tunnel. These vessels, called spiral vessels, do not enter the organ of Corti but are thought to supply most of the oxygen and other nutrients to its cells. Although the outer spiral vessel is seldom found in adult animals of certain species such as the dog, cat, and rat and is not found in the basilar membrane of every adult human, it is present in the human fetus. Its impressive diameter in the fetus suggests that it is an important channel for blood delivery to the developing organ of Corti.

Organ of Corti

Arranged on the surface of the basilar membrane are orderly rows of the sensory hair cells, which generate nerve impulses in response to sound vibrations. Together with their supporting cells they form a complex neuroepithelium called the basilar papilla, or organ of Corti. The organ of Corti is named after Italian anatomist Alfonso Corti, who first described it in 1851. Viewed in cross section the most striking feature of the organ of Corti is the arch, or tunnel, of Corti, formed by two rows of pillar cells, or rods. The pillar cells furnish the major support of this

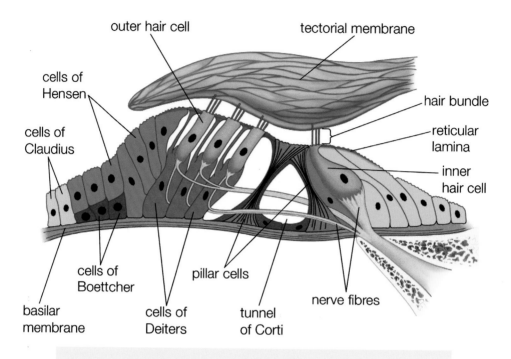

Structure of the organ of Corti. Encyclopædia Britannica, Inc.

structure. They separate a single row of larger, pear-shaped, inner hair cells from three or more rows of smaller, cylindrical, outer hair cells. The inner hair cells are supported and enclosed by the inner phalangeal, cells, which rest on the thin outer portion, called the tympanic lip, of the spiral limbus. On the inner side of the inner hair cells and the cells that support them is a curved furrow called the inner sulcus. This is lined with more or less undifferentiated cuboidal cells.

Each outer hair cell is supported by a phalangeal cell of Deiters, which holds the base of the hair cell in a cup-shaped depression. From each Deiters' cell a projection extends upward to the stiff membrane, the reticular lamina, that covers the organ of Corti. The top of the hair cell is firmly held by the lamina, but the body is suspended in fluid that fills the space of Nuel and the tunnel of Corti. Although this fluid is sometimes referred to as cortilymph, its composition is thought to be similar, if not identical, to that of the perilymph. Beyond the hair cells and the Deiters' cells are three other types of epithelial cells, usually called the cells of Hensen, Claudius, and Boettcher, after the 19th-century anatomists who first described them. Their function has not been established, but they are assumed to help in maintaining the composition of the endolymph by ion transport and absorptive activity.

Each hair cell has a cytoskeleton composed of filaments of the protein actin, which imparts stiffness to structures in which it is found. The hair cell is capped by a dense cuticular plate, composed of actin filaments, which bears a tuft of stiffly erect stereocilia, also containing actin, of graded lengths arranged in a staircase pattern. This so-called hair bundle has rootlets anchored firmly in the cuticular plate. On the top of the inner hair cells 40 to 60 stereocilia are arranged in two or more irregularly parallel rows. On the outer hair cells approximately 100 stereocilia form a W pattern. At the notch of the W the plate is incomplete, with only a thin cell membrane taking its place. Beneath the membrane is the basal body of a kinocilium, although no motile ciliary (hairlike) portion is present as is the case on the hair cells of the vestibular system.

The stereocilia are about three to five micrometres in length. The longest make contact with but do not penetrate the tectorial membrane. This membrane is an acellular, gelatinous structure that covers the top of the spiral limbus as a thin fibrillar layer, then becomes thicker as it extends outward over the inner sulcus and the reticular lamina. Its fibrils extend radially and somewhat obliquely to end at its lateral border, just above the junction of the reticular lamina and the cells of Hensen. In the upper turns of the cochlea, the margin of the membrane ends in fingerlike projections that make contact with the stereocilia of the outermost hair cells.

The myelin-ensheathed fibres of the vestibulocochlear nerve fan out in spiral fashion from the modiolus to pass into the channel near the root of the osseous spiral lamina, called the canal of Rosenthal. The bipolar cell bodies of these neurons constitute the spiral ganglion. Beyond the ganglion their distal processes extend radially outward in the bony lamina beneath the limbus to pass through an array of small pores directly under the inner hair cells, called the habenula perforata. Here the fibres abruptly lose their multilayered coats of myelin (a substance that insulates long sections of nerve cells called axons) and continue as thin, naked, unmyelinated fibres into the organ of Corti. Some fibres form a longitudinally directed bundle running beneath the inner hair cells and another bundle just inside the tunnel, above the feet of the inner pillar cells. The majority of the fibres (some 95 percent in the human ear) end on the inner hair cells. The remainder cross the tunnel to form longitudinal bundles beneath the rows of the outer hair cells on which they eventually terminate.

The endings of the nerve fibres beneath the hair cells are of two distinct types. The larger and more numerous endings contain many minute vesicles, or liquid-filled sacs, containing neurotransmitters, which mediate impulse transmission at neural junctions. These endings belong to a special bundle of nerve fibres that arise in the brainstem and constitute an efferent system, or feedback loop, to the cochlea. The smaller and less numerous endings contain

few vesicles or other cell structures. They are the termina-
tions of the afferent fibres of the cochlear nerve, which
transmit impulses from the hair cells to the brainstem.

The total number of outer hair cells in the cochlea has
been estimated at 12,000 and the number of inner hair
cells at 3,500. Although there are about 30,000 fibres in
the cochlear nerve, there is considerable overlap in the
innervation of the outer hair cells. A single fibre may supply endings to many hair cells, which thus share a "party
line." Furthermore, a single hair cell may receive nerve
endings from many fibres. The actual distribution of nerve
fibres in the organ of Corti has not been worked out in
detail, but it is known that the inner hair cells receive the
lion's share of afferent fibre endings without the overlap-
ping and sharing of fibres that are characteristic of the
outer hair cells.

Viewed from above, the organ of Corti with its covering, the reticular lamina, forms a well-defined mosaic
pattern. In humans the arrangement of the outer hair
cells in the basal turn of the cochlea is quite regular, with
three distinct and orderly rows. In the higher turns of
the cochlea, however, the arrangement becomes slightly
irregular, as scattered cells form fourth or fifth rows.
The spaces between the outer hair cells are filled by
oddly shaped extensions (phalangeal plates) of the supporting cells. The double row of head plates of the inner
and outer pillar cells cover the tunnel and separate the
inner from the outer hair cells. The reticular lamina
extends from the inner border cells near the inner sulcus
to the Hensen cells but does not include either of these
cell groups. When a hair cell degenerates and disappears
as a result of aging, disease, or noise-induced injury, its
place is quickly covered by the adjacent phalangeal
plates, which expand to form an easily recognized "scar."

ENDOLYMPH AND PERILYMPH

The perilymph, which fills the space within the bony labyrinth surrounding the membranous labyrinth, is similar, but not identical, in composition to other extracellular fluids of the body, such as cerebrospinal fluid. The concentration of sodium ions in the perilymph is high (about 150 milliequivalents per litre), and that of potassium ions is low (about 5 milliequivalents per litre), as is true of other extracellular fluids. Like these fluids, the perilymph is apparently formed locally from the blood plasma by transport mechanisms that selectively allow substances to cross the walls of the capillaries. Although it is anatomically possible for cerebrospinal fluid to enter the cochlea by way of the perilymphatic duct, experimental studies have made it appear unlikely that the cerebrospinal fluid is involved in the normal production of perilymph.

The membranous labyrinth is filled with endolymph, which is unique among extracellular fluids of the body, including the perilymph, in that its potassium ion concentration is higher (about 140 milliequivalents per litre) than its sodium ion concentration (about 15 milliequivalents per litre).

The process of formation of the endolymph and the maintenance of the difference in ionic composition between it and perilymph are not yet completely understood. Reissner's membrane forms a selective barrier between the two fluids. Blood-endolymph and blood-perilymph barriers, which control the passage of substances such as drugs from the blood to the inner ear, appear to exist as well. Evidence indicates that the endolymph is produced from perilymph as a result of selective ion transport through the epithelial cells of Reissner's membrane and not directly from the blood. The secretory tissue called the stria vascularis, in the lateral wall of the cochlear duct, is thought to play an important role in maintaining the high ratio of potassium ions to sodium ions in the endolymph. Other tissues of the cochlea, as well as the dark cells of the vestibular organs, which must produce their own endolymph, are also thought to be involved in maintaining the ionic composition of the endolymph.

Because the membranous labyrinth is a closed system, the questions of flow and removal of the endolymph are also important. The endolymph is thought to be reabsorbed from the endolymphatic sac, although this appears to be only part of the story. Other cochlear and vestibular tissues may also have important roles in regulating the volume and maintaining the composition of the inner-ear fluids.

CHAPTER 2

HEARING AND BALANCE

The key functions of the ear—hearing and balance—are made possible by the organ's unique anatomical and physiological arrangement. The outer ear, for example, directs sound waves toward the inner ear, where vibrations are converted into electrochemical impulses that travel along the cochlear nerve to the brainstem and into the brain's sound-processing centre, the auditory nucleus. Likewise, information about the position or orientation of the head and body with respect to gravity is conveyed to the sensory hair cells of the inner ear by the pressure of the otoliths. This pressure results in the relay of nerve impulses from the inner ear, along the vestibular nerve, to the brainstem and cerebellum. Balance signals received by the brain are then relayed to the trunk and limbs of the body, enabling adjustment of posture and position. Input from the eyes assists in fine-tuning these adjustments.

THE PHYSIOLOGY OF HEARING

Hearing is the process by which the ear transforms sound vibrations in the external environment into nerve impulses that are conveyed to the brain, where they are interpreted as sounds. Sounds are produced when vibrating objects, such as the plucked string of a guitar, produce pressure pulses of vibrating air molecules, better known as sound waves.

The ear can distinguish different subjective aspects of a sound, such as its loudness and pitch, by detecting and analyzing different physical characteristics of the waves. Pitch is the perception of the frequency of sound waves — i.e., the number of wavelengths that pass a fixed point in a unit of time. Frequency is usually measured in cycles per second, or hertz. The human ear is most sensitive to and most easily detects frequencies of 1,000 to 4,000 hertz, but at least for normal young ears the entire audible range of sounds extends from about 20 to 20,000 hertz. Sound waves of still higher frequency are referred to as ultrasonic, although they can be heard by other mammals.

Loudness is the perception of the intensity of sound — i.e., the pressure exerted by sound waves on the tympanic membrane. The greater their amplitude or strength, the greater is the pressure or intensity, and consequently the loudness, of the sound. The intensity of sound is measured and reported in decibels (dB), a unit that expresses the relative magnitude of a sound on a logarithmic scale. Stated in another way, the decibel is a unit for comparing the intensity of any given sound with a standard sound that is just perceptible to the normal human ear at a frequency in the range to which the ear is most sensitive. On the decibel scale, the range of human hearing extends from 0 decibels, which represents a level that is all but inaudible, to about 130 decibels, the level at which sound becomes painful.

In order for a sound to be transmitted to the central nervous system, the energy of the sound undergoes three transformations. First, the air vibrations are converted to vibrations of the tympanic membrane and ossicles of the middle ear. These, in turn, become vibrations in the fluid within the cochlea. Finally, the fluid vibrations set up traveling waves along the basilar membrane that stimulate the hair cells of the organ of Corti. These cells convert the sound vibrations to nerve impulses in the fibres of the cochlear nerve, which transmits them to the brainstem, from which they are relayed, after extensive processing, to

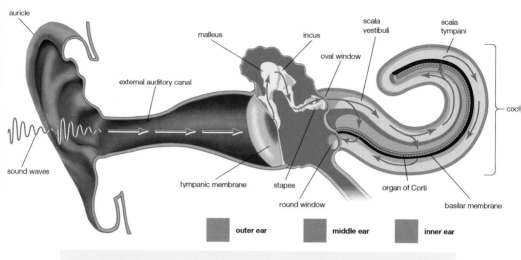

The mechanism of hearing. Sound waves enter the outer ear and travel through the external auditory canal until they reach the tympanic membrane, causing the membrane and the attached chain of auditory ossicles to vibrate. The motion of the stapes against the oval window sets up waves in the fluids of the cochlea, causing the basilar membrane to vibrate. This stimulates the sensory cells of the organ of Corti, atop the basilar membrane, to send nerve impulses to the brain. Encyclopædia Britannica, Inc.

the primary auditory area of the cerebral cortex, the ultimate centre of the brain for hearing. Only when the nerve impulses reach this area does the listener become aware of the sound.

TRANSMISSION OF SOUND WAVES THROUGH THE OUTER AND MIDDLE EAR

Before nerve impulses carrying information about sound are generated and relayed to the brain, the sound waves are first captured by the outer ear and transmitted through the middle ear. The different structural features of the outer and middle ear contribute in various ways to the transmission of sound, and collectively they serve a remarkable role in hearing.

Transmission of Sound by Air Conduction

The outer ear directs sound waves from the external environment to the tympanic membrane. The auricle, the visible portion of the outer ear, collects sound waves and, with the concha, the cavity at the entrance to the external auditory canal, helps to funnel sound into the canal. Because of its small size and virtual immobility, the auricle in humans is less useful in sound gathering and direction finding than it is in many animals. The canal helps to enhance the amount of sound that reaches the tympanic membrane. This resonance enhancement works only for sounds of relatively short wavelength—those in the frequency range between 2,000 and 7,000 hertz—which helps to determine the frequencies to which the ear is most sensitive, those important for distinguishing the sounds of consonants.

Sounds reaching the tympanic membrane are in part reflected and in part absorbed. Only absorbed sound sets the membrane in motion. The tendency of the ear to oppose the passage of sound is called acoustic impedance. The magnitude of the impedance depends on the mass and stiffness of the membrane and the ossicular chain and on the frictional resistance they offer.

When the tympanic membrane absorbs sound waves, its central portion, the umbo, vibrates as a stiff cone, bending inward and outward. The greater the force of the sound waves, the greater the deflection of the membrane and the louder the sound. The higher the frequency of a sound, the faster the membrane vibrates and the higher the pitch of the sound is. The motion of the membrane is transferred to the handle of the malleus, the tip of which is attached at the umbo. At higher frequencies the motion of the membrane is no longer simple, and transmission to the malleus may be somewhat less effective.

The malleus and incus are suspended by small elastic ligaments and are finely balanced, with their masses evenly distributed above and below their common axis of rotation. The head of the malleus and the body of the incus are tightly bound together, with the result that they move as a unit in unison with the tympanic membrane. At moderate sound pressures, the vibrations are passed on to the stapes, and the whole ossicular chain moves as a single mass. However, there may be considerable freedom of motion and some loss of energy at the joint between the incus and the stapes because of their relatively loose coupling. The stapes does not move in and out but rocks back and forth about the lower pole of its footplate, which impinges on the membrane covering the oval window in the bony plate of the inner ear. The action of the stapes transmits the sound waves to the perilymph of the vestibule and the scala vestibuli.

Function of the Ossicular Chain

In order for sound to be transmitted to the inner ear, the vibrations in the air must be changed to vibrations in the cochlear fluids. There is a challenge involved in this task that has to do with difference in impedance—the resistance to the passage of sound—between air and fluid. This difference, or mismatch, of impedances reduces the transmission of sound. The tympanic membrane and the ossicles function to overcome the mismatch of impedances between air and the cochlear fluids, and thus the middle ear serves as a transformer, or impedance matching device.

Ordinarily, when airborne sound strikes the surface of a body of water, almost all of its energy is reflected and only about 0.1 percent passes into the water. In the ear this would represent a transmission loss of 30 decibels, enough to seriously limit the ear's performance, were it not for the transformer action of the middle ear. The matching of impedances is accomplished in two ways, primarily by the reduction in area between the tympanic membrane and the stapes footplate and secondarily by the mechanical advantage of the lever formed by the malleus and incus. Although the total area of the tympanic membrane is about 69 square millimetres (0.1 square inch), the area of its central portion that is free to move has been estimated at about 43 square millimetres. The sound energy that causes this area of the membrane to vibrate is transmitted and concentrated in the 3.2-square-millimetre area of the stapes footplate. Thus, the pressure is increased at least 13 times. The mechanical advantage of the ossicular lever (which exists because the handle of the malleus is longer than the long projection of the incus) amounts to about 1.3. The total increase in pressure at the footplate is, therefore, not less than 17-fold, depending on the area of the tympanic membrane that is actually vibrating. At frequencies in the range of 3,000 to 5,000 hertz, the increase may be even greater because of the resonant properties of the ear canal.

The ossicular chain not only concentrates sound in a small area but also applies sound preferentially to one window of the cochlea, the oval window. If the oval and round windows were exposed equally to airborne sound crossing the middle ear, the vibrations in the perilymph of the scala vestibuli would be opposed by those in the perilymph of the scala tympani, and little effective movement of the basilar membrane would result. As it is, sound is delivered selectively to the oval window, and the round window moves in reciprocal fashion, bulging outward in response to an inward movement of the stapes footplate and inward when the stapes moves away from the oval window. The passage of vibrations through the air across the middle ear from the tympanic membrane to the round window is of negligible importance.

Thanks to these mechanical features of the middle ear, the hair cells of the normal cochlea are able to respond, at the threshold of hearing for frequencies to which the ear is most sensitive, to vibrations of the tympanic membrane on the order of 1 angstrom (0.0000001 mm) in amplitude. On the other hand, when the ossicular chain is immobilized by disease, as in otosclerosis, which causes the stapes footplate to become fixed in the oval window, the threshold of hearing may increase by as much as 60 decibels (1,000-fold), which represents a significant degree of impairment. Bypassing the ossicular chain through the surgical creation of a new window can restore hearing to within 25 to 30 decibels of the normal. Only if the fixed stapes is removed (stapedectomy) and replaced by a tiny artificial stapes can normal hearing be approached. Fortunately, operations performed on the middle ear have been perfected so that defects causing conductive impairment often can be corrected and a useful level of hearing restored.

Function of the Muscles of the Middle Ear

The muscles of the middle ear, the tensor tympani and the stapedius, can influence the transmission of sound by the ossicular chain. Contraction of the tensor tympani pulls the handle of the malleus inward and, as the name of the muscle suggests, tenses the tympanic membrane. Contraction of the stapedius pulls the stapes footplate outward from the oval window and thereby reduces the intensity of sound reaching the cochlea. The stapedius responds reflexly with quick contraction to sounds of high intensity applied either to the same ear or to the opposite ear. The reflex has been likened to the blink of the eye or the constriction of the pupil of the eye in response to light and is thought to have protective value. Unfortunately, the contractions of the middle-ear muscles are not instantaneous, so that they do not protect the cochlea against damage by sudden intense noise, such as that of an explosion or of gunfire. They also fatigue rather quickly and thus offer little protection against injury sustained from high-level noise, such as that experienced in rock concerts and many industrial workplaces.

Transmission of Sound by Bone Conduction

There is another route by which sound can reach the inner ear: by conduction through the bones of the skull. When the handle of a vibrating tuning fork is placed on a bony prominence such as the forehead or mastoid process behind the ear, its note is clearly audible. Similarly, the ticking of a watch held between the teeth can be distinctly heard. When the external canals are closed with the fingers, the sound becomes louder, indicating that it is not entering the ear by the usual channel. Instead, it is producing vibrations of the skull that are passed on to the inner ear, either directly or indirectly, through the bone.

The higher audible frequencies cause the skull to vibrate in segments, and these vibrations are transmitted to the cochlear fluids by direct compression of the otic capsule, the bony case enclosing the inner ear. Because the round window membrane is more freely mobile than the stapes footplate, the vibrations set up in the perilymph of the scala vestibuli are not canceled out by those in the scala tympani, and the resultant movements of the basilar membrane can stimulate the organ of Corti. This type of transmission is known as compression bone conduction.

At lower frequencies—i.e., 1,500 hertz and below—the skull moves as a rigid body. The ossicles are less affected and move less freely than the cochlea and the margins of the oval window because of their inertia, their suspension in the middle-ear cavity, and their loose coupling to the skull. The result is that the oval window moves with respect to the footplate of the stapes, which gives the same effect as if the stapes itself were vibrating. This form of transmission is known as inertial bone conduction. In otosclerosis the fixed stapes interferes with inertial, but not with compressional, bone conduction.

In persons with middle-ear disease, hearing aids with special vibrators are sometimes used to deliver sound to the mastoid process (the part of the temporal bone behind the ear), which is then conducted by bone to the inner ear. Bone conduction is also the basis of some of the oldest, simplest, and most useful tests in the repertoire of the otologist. These tests employ tuning forks to distinguish between conductive impairment, which affects the middle ear and is amenable to surgery, and sensorineural impairment, which affects the inner ear and the cochlear nerve and for which surgery usually is not indicated.

TRANSMISSION OF SOUND WITHIN THE INNER EAR

Within the inner ear, the mechanical vibrations produced by sound waves are transduced into electrochemical signals. This process of conversion occurs specifically in the organ of Corti, which contains hair cell nerve fibres that are sensitive to vibration. When triggered beyond a certain threshold, the hair cells send out pulses of voltage that travel along the fibres and are transmitted to con-

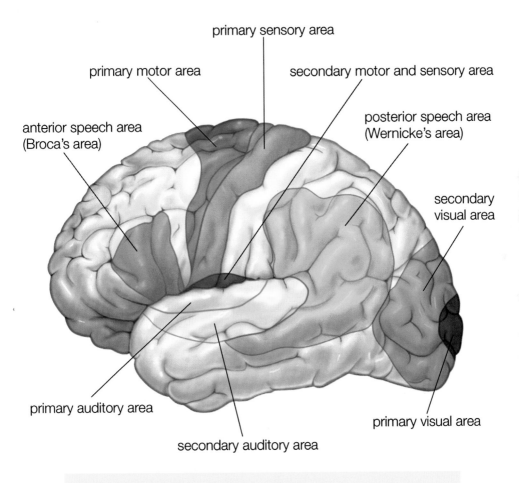

primary sensory area

primary motor area

secondary motor and sensory area

posterior speech area
(Wernicke's area)

anterior speech area
(Broca's area)

secondary
visual area

primary auditory area

primary visual area

secondary auditory area

Functional areas of the human brain. Encyclopædia Britannica, Inc.

necting neurons, thereby facilitating the rapid relay of the pulses to the auditory nucleus in the brain.

Transmission of Sound Waves in the Cochlea

The mechanical vibrations of the stapes footplate at the oval window creates pressure waves in the perilymph of the scala vestibuli of the cochlea. These waves move around the tip of the cochlea through the helicotrema into the scala tympani and dissipate as they hit the round window. The wave motion is transmitted to the endolymph inside the cochlear duct. As a result the basilar membrane vibrates, which causes the organ of Corti to move against the tectoral membrane, stimulating generation of nerve impulses to the brain.

The vibrations of the stapes footplate against the oval window do not affect the semicircular canals or the utricle of the vestibular system unless middle-ear disease has eroded the bony wall of the lateral canal and produced an abnormal opening. In such a case loud sounds may cause transient vertigo (the Tullio phenomenon). However, laboratory evidence suggests that the saccule of mammals may retain some degree of responsiveness to intense sound, an intriguing observation because the saccule is the organ of hearing in fish, the distant ancestors of mammals. Normally only the cochlear fluids and the cochlear duct vibrate in response to alternating pressures at the oval window, because only the cochlea has the round window as a "relief valve."

Within the cochlea the different frequencies of complex sounds are sorted out, or analyzed, and the physical energy of these sound vibrations is converted, or transduced, into electrical impulses that are transmitted to the brainstem by the cochlear nerve. The cochlea analyzes sound frequencies (distinguishes pitch) by means of the basilar membrane, which exhibits different degrees of stiffness, or resonance, along its length.

The idea of the ear as a multiresonant structure was proposed by several anatomists in the 17th and 18th centuries. In the late 19th century German physicist and physiologist Hermann von Helmholtz explicitly stated these ideas in his resonance theory of hearing. Inspired by the anatomic studies of the cochlea by Alfonso Corti,

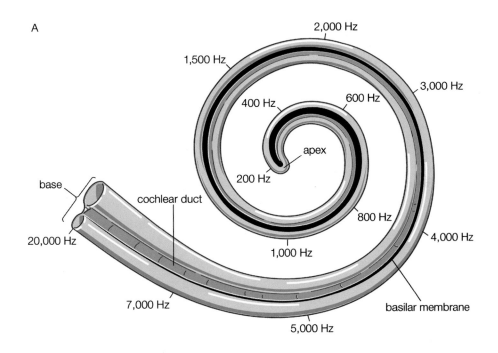

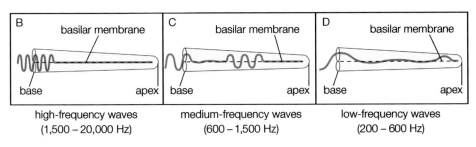

The analysis of sound frequencies by the basilar membrane. (A) The fibres of the basilar membrane become progressively wider and more flexible from the base of the cochlea to the apex. As a result, each area of the basilar membrane vibrates preferentially to a particular sound frequency. (B) High-frequency sound waves cause maximum vibration of the area of the basilar membrane nearest to the base of the cochlea; (C) medium-frequency waves affect the centre of the membrane; (D) and low-frequency waves preferentially stimulate the apex of the basilar membrane. (The locations of cochlear frequencies along the basilar membrane shown are a composite drawn from different sources.)
Encyclopædia Britannica, Inc.

Helmholtz postulated that there was a series of resonators in the cochlea capable of analyzing complex sounds into their component frequencies. After examining various structures of the inner ear, he identified the resonators to be fibres that span the basilar membrane. The fibres vary in length like piano strings, increasing progressively from the basal end of the basilar membrane to the apex at the tip of the cochlea. Helmholtz conjectured that the length of the fibres tunes them to vibrate at specific frequencies. Although in its original form Helmholtz' resonance theory is no longer accepted, clinical and experimental data support the closely related "place theory," which holds that sounds of different frequency activate different regions of the basilar membrane and organ of Corti.

Subsequent experiments carried out in the 20th century by Hungarian-born American physicist and physiologist Georg von Békésy have shown that the way in which the cochlea analyzes frequency, or distinguishes pitch, does not occur because of a series of separately tuned resonators, as Helmholtz theorized. Instead, pitch is distinguished because of the continuous changes that occur along the length of the basilar membrane, which increases in width and mass and decreases in stiffness from its base near the oval window to its apex. Each region of the membrane is most affected by a specific frequency of vibrations. Low-frequency sounds cause the apical end of the membrane to vibrate, and high-frequency sounds cause the basal end to vibrate. Vibrations reaching the basal end through the perilymph proceed along the membrane as traveling waves that attain their maximum amplitude at a distance corresponding to their frequency and then rapidly subside. The higher the frequency of the sound imposed, the shorter the distance the waves travel. Thus, a tone of a given frequency causes stimulation to reach a peak at a certain place on the basilar membrane.

The region that vibrates most vigorously stimulates the greatest number of hair cells in that area of the organ of Corti, and these hair cells send the most nerve impulses to the auditory nerve and the brain. The brain recognizes the place on the basilar membrane and thus the pitch of the tone by the particular group of nerve fibres activated. For the lower frequencies—up to about 3,000 hertz—the rate of stimulation is also an important indicator of pitch. This means that the auditory nerve fibres convey information to the brain about the timing of the sound frequency as well as its place of maximum vibration on the membrane. For higher frequencies place alone seems to be decisive.

Loudness also is determined at this level by the amplitude, or height, of the vibration of the basilar membrane. As a sound increases, so does the amplitude of the vibration. This increases both the number of hair cells stimulated and the rate at which they generate nerve impulses.

Transduction of Mechanical Vibrations

The hair cells located in the organ of Corti transduce mechanical sound vibrations into nerve impulses. They are stimulated when the basilar membrane, on which the organ of Corti rests, vibrates. The hair cells are held in place by the reticular lamina, a rigid structure supported by the pillar cells, or rods of Corti, which are attached to the basilar fibres. At the base of the hair cells is a network of cochlear nerve endings, which lead to the spiral ganglion of Corti in the modiolus of the cochlea. The spiral ganglion sends axons into the cochlear nerve. At the top of the hair cell is a hair bundle containing stereocilia, or sensory hairs, that project upward into the tectorial membrane, which lies above the stereocilia in the cochlear duct. (The single kinocilium, which is found on the hair cells of the vestibular system, is not found on the receptor cells of the cochlea.) When the basilar membrane moves upward, the reticular lamina moves upward and inward. When the membrane moves downward, the reticular lamina moves downward and outward. The resultant shearing forces between the reticular lamina and the tectorial membrane displace or bend the longest of the stereocilia, exciting the nerve fibres at the base of the hair cells.

The mechanism the hair cell uses to convert sound into an electrical stimulus is not completely understood, but certain key features are known. One of the most important aspects of this process is the endocochlear potential, which exists between the endolymph and perilymph. This direct current potential difference is about +80 millivolts and results from the difference in potassium content between the two fluids. It is thought to be maintained by the continual transport of potassium ions from the perilymph into the cochlear duct by the stria vascularis. The endolymph, which has a high potassium level and a positive potential, is contained in the cochlear duct and thus bathes the tops of the hair cells. The perilymph, which has a low potassium level and a negative potential, is contained in the scala vestibuli and scala tympani and bathes the lower parts of the hair cells. The inside of the hair cell has a negative intracellular potential of -60 millivolts with respect to the perilymph and -140 millivolts with respect to the endolymph. This rather steep gradient, especially at the tip of the cell, is thought to sensitize the cell to the slightest sound.

The stereocilia are graded in height, becoming longer on the side away from the modiolus. All the stereocilia are interlinked so that, when the taller ones are moved against the tectorial membrane, the shorter ones move as well. The mechanical movement of this hair bundle generates an alternating hair cell receptor potential. This occurs in the following manner. When the stereocilia are bent in the direction of increasing stereocilia length, ion channels in the membrane open, allowing potassium ions to move into the cell. The influx of potassium ions excites, or depolarizes, the hair cell. However, when the stereocilia are deflected in the opposite direction, the ion channels are shut and the hair cell is inhibited, or hyperpolarized. The depolarization of the cell stimulates the release of chemicals called neurotransmitters from the base of the hair cell. The neurotransmitters are absorbed by the nerve fibres located at the basal end of the hair cell, stimulating them to send an electrical signal along the cochlear nerve.

The outer hair cells contain both actin and myosin, the same contractile proteins that make up muscles, and this allows the cells to contract rhythmically in response to tonal stimuli. Recent studies suggest that the cells themselves may be tuned structures. The ability of an outer hair cell to respond to a particular frequency may depend not only on its position along the length of the basilar membrane but also on its mechanical resonance, which probably varies with the length of its bundle of stereocilia and with that of its cell body. The inner hair cells are much more uniform in size. Local groups of outer hair cells act not only as detectors of low-level sound stimuli, but, because they can act as mechanical-electrical stimulators and feedback elements, they are believed to modify and enhance the discriminatory responses of the inner hair cells. How they do this is not understood. Because the inner hair cells rest on the bony shelf of the osseous spiral lamina rather than on the basilar membrane, they are presumably less readily stimulated by the traveling wave. Help from the outer hair cells may be required to generate the signal that the inner cells transmit synaptically to the fibres of the cochlear nerve. Experiments in animals have shown that, when the outer hair cells of the basal turn have been destroyed by the ototoxic action of the antibiotic kanamycin, the inner hair cells in the same region can still respond to sound, but their thresholds are elevated by about 40 decibels.

Remarkably, the cochlea itself actually produces sounds. Its otacoustic emissions can be spontaneous or evoked by external acoustic stimulation. These emissions are thought to be produced by rhythmical contractions of the cochlear hair cells. Although faint, they can be recorded with a small microphone placed in the external canal. They are absent when there has been extensive loss of hair cells from the basal turn, as in cases of presbycusis or ototoxicity. While these emissions challenge some earlier concepts of the micromechanisms of cochlear function, they are proving increasingly useful in the audiological evaluation of impaired hearing, in adults as well as infants.

COCHLEAR NERVE AND CENTRAL AUDITORY PATHWAYS

The fibre of hearing and balance is the vestibulocochlear nerve, which consists of two anatomically and functionally distinct parts: the cochlear (or auditory) nerve and the vestibular nerve. The cochlear branch innervates the organ of hearing and ultimately communicates with the auditory nucleus of the brain. The neural tracts that it follows to and from the brain—its ascending and descending pathways, respectively—are well characterized. The cochlear nerve and its pathways are discussed in detail here.

Auditory Nerve Fibres

The fibres of the cochlear nerve originate from an aggregation of nerve cell bodies, the spiral ganglion, located in the modiolus of the cochlea. The neurons of the spiral ganglion are called bipolar cells because they have two sets of processes, or fibres, that extend from opposite ends of the cell body. The longer, central fibres, also called the primary auditory fibres, form the cochlear nerve, and the shorter, peripheral fibres extend to the bases of the inner and outer hair cells. They extend radially from the spiral ganglion to the habenula perforata, a series of tiny holes beneath the inner hair cells. At this point they lose their myelin sheaths and enter the organ of Corti as thin, unmyelinated fibres. There are only about 30,000 of these fibres, and the greater number of them—about 95 percent—innervate the inner hair cells. The remainder cross the tunnel of Corti to innervate the outer hair cells. The longer central processes of the bipolar cochlear neurons unite and are twisted like the cords of a rope to form the cochlear nerve trunk. These primary auditory fibres exit the modiolus through the internal meatus, or passageway, and immediately enter the part of the brainstem called the medulla.

Ascending Auditory Pathways

The central auditory pathways extend from the medulla to the cerebral cortex. They consist of a series of nuclei (groups of nerve cell bodies in the central nervous system similar to a peripheral ganglion) connected by fibre tracts made up of their axons (processes that convey signals away from the cell bodies). This complex chain of nerve cells helps to process and relay auditory information, encoded in the form of nerve impulses, directly to the highest cerebral levels in the cortex of the brain. To some extent different properties of the auditory stimulus are conveyed along distinct parallel pathways. This method of transmission, employed by other sensory systems, provides a means for the central nervous system to analyze different properties of the single auditory stimulus, with some information processed at low levels and other information at higher levels. At lower levels of the pathway, information as to pitch, loudness, and localization of sounds is processed, and appropriate responses, such as the contraction of the intra-aural muscles, turning of the eyes and head, or movements of the body as a whole, are initiated.

In the medulla the fibres of the cochlear nerve terminate when they reach a collection of nerve cells called the cochlear nucleus. The cochlear nucleus consists of several distinct cell types and is divided into the dorsal and ventral (back and front) cochlear nucleus. Each cochlear nerve fibre branches at the cochlear nucleus, sending one branch to the dorsal and the other branch to the ventral cochlear nucleus.

Some fibres from the ventral cochlear nucleus pass across the midline to the cells of the superior olivary complex, whereas others make connection with the olivary cells of the same side. Together, these fibres form the trapezoid body. Fibres from the dorsal cochlear nucleus cross the midline to end on the cells of the nuclei of the lateral lemniscus. There they are joined by the fibres from the ventral cochlear nuclei of both sides and from the olivary complex. The lemniscus is a major tract, most of the fibres of which end in the inferior colliculus, the auditory centre of the midbrain, although some fibres may bypass the colliculus and end, together with the fibres from the colliculus, at the next higher level, the medial geniculate body. From the medial geniculate body there is an orderly projection of fibres to a portion of the cortex of the temporal lobe.

In humans and other primates the primary acoustic area in the cerebral cortex is the superior transverse temporal gyri of Heschl, a ridge in the temporal lobe, on the lower lip of the deep cleft between the temporal and parietal lobes, known as the sylvian fissure.

Because about half of the fibres of the auditory pathways cross the midline while others ascend on the same side of the brain, each ear is represented in both the right and left cortex. For this reason, even when the auditory cortical area of one side is injured by trauma or stroke, binaural hearing may be little affected. Impaired hearing due to bilateral cortical injury involving both auditory areas has been reported, but it is extremely rare.

Descending Auditory Pathways

Parallel with the pathway ascending from the cochlear nuclei to the cortex is a pathway descending from the cortex to the cochlear nuclei. In both pathways some of the fibres remain on the same side, while others cross the midline to the opposite side of the brain. There is also evidence of a "spur" line ascending from the dorsal cochlear nucleus to the cerebellum and another descending from the inferior colliculus to the cerebellum. The significance of these cerebral connections is not clear, but they may antedate the evolutionary development of the cerebral cortex. In general, the descending fibres may be regarded as exercising an inhibitory function by means of a sort of "negative feedback." They also may determine which ascending impulses are to be blocked and which are allowed to pass on to the higher centres of the brain.

From the superior olivary complex, a region in the medulla oblongata at the base of the brainstem, there arises a fibre tract called the olivocochlear bundle. It constitutes an efferent system, or feedback loop, by which nerve impulses, thought to be inhibitory, reach the hair cells. This

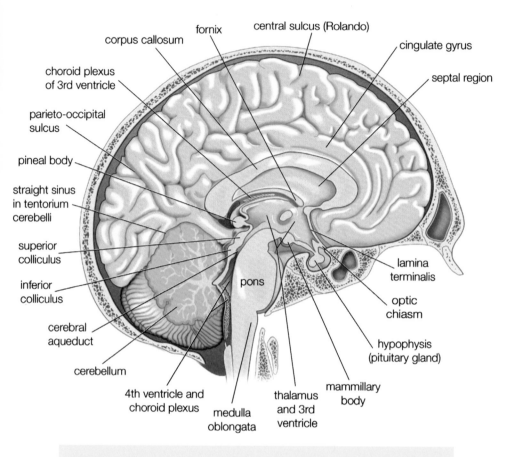

Medial view of the left hemisphere of the human brain. Encyclopædia Britannica, Inc.

system, which uses acetylcholine as a neurotransmitter, is presumably involved in sharpening, or otherwise modifying, the analysis that is made in the cochlea.

ANALYSIS OF SOUND BY THE AUDITORY NERVOUS SYSTEM

Evidence of orderly spatial representations of the organ of Corti at the lower levels of the auditory pathway has been reported by many investigators. These patterns seem to be in accord with the place theory of the cochlear analysis of sound. Physiological evidence of tuning of the auditory system also has been obtained by recording with the electrical potentials from individual neurons at various levels. Most neurons of the auditory pathway show a "best frequency"—i.e., a frequency to which the individual neuron responds at minimal intensity. This finding is entirely compatible with experimental evidence of frequency tuning of the hair cells. With each increase in the intensity of the sound stimulus, the neuron is able to respond to a wider band of frequencies, thus reflecting the broad tuning of the basilar membrane. With sounds of lower frequency, the rate of impulses fired by the neuron reflects the stimulus frequency, and the response often reveals phase-locking with the stimulus. In other words, the nerve fibres are stimulated at regularly recurring intervals, corresponding to a particular position or phase, of each sound wave. Increased intensity of stimulation causes a more rapid rate of responding. In general, the pitch of a sound tends to be coded in terms of which neurons are responding, and its loudness is determined by the rate of response and the total number of neurons activated.

Although extensive studies have been made of the responses of single cortical neurons, the data do not yet fit any comprehensive theory of auditory analysis. Experiments in animals have indicated that the cortex is not even necessary for frequency recognition, which can be carried out at lower levels, but that it is essential for the recognition of temporal patterns of sound. It appears likely, therefore, that in humans the cortex is reserved for the analysis of more complex auditory stimuli, such as speech and music, for which the temporal sequence of sounds is equally important.

Presumably it is also at the cortical level that the meaning of sounds is interpreted and behaviour is adjusted in accordance with their significance. Such functions were formerly attributed to an "auditory association area" immediately surrounding the primary area, but they probably should be thought of as involving much more of the cerebral cortex, thanks to the multiple, parallel interconnections between the various areas.

The localization of sounds from a stationary source in the horizontal plane is known to depend on the recognition of minute differences in the intensity and time of arrival of the sound at the two ears. A sound that arrives at the right ear a few microseconds sooner than it does at the left or that sounds a few decibels louder in that ear is recognized as coming from the right. In a real-life situation the head may also be turned to pinpoint the sound by facing it and thus canceling these differences. For low-frequency tones a difference in phase at the two ears is the criterion for localization, but for higher frequencies the difference in loudness caused by the sound shadow of the head becomes all-important. Such comparisons and discriminations appear to be carried out at brainstem and midbrain levels of the central auditory pathway. The spectral shapes of sounds have been shown to be most important for determining the elevation of a source that is not in the horizontal plane. Localization of sound that emanates from a moving source is a more complicated task for the nervous system and apparently involves the cerebral cortex and short-term memory. Experiments in animals have shown that injury to the auditory area of the cortex on one side of the brain interferes with the localization of a moving sound source on the opposite side of the body.

Each cochlear nucleus receives impulses only from the ear of the same side. A comparison between the responses of the two ears first becomes possible at the superior oli-vary complex, which receives fibres from both cochlear nuclei. Electrophysiological experiments in animals have shown that some neurons of the accessory nucleus of the olivary complex respond to impulses from both ears. Others respond to impulses from one side exclusively, but their response is modified by the simultaneous arrival of impulses from the other side.

The system appears to be capable of making the extraordinarily fine discriminations of time and intensity that are necessary for sound localization. By virtue of such bilateral neural interconnections in the brain, the two ears together can be much more effective than one ear alone in picking out a particular sound in the presence of a background of noise. They also permit attention to be directed to a single source of sound, such as one instru-ment in an orchestra or one voice in a crowd. This is one aspect of the "cocktail party effect," whereby a listener with normal hearing can attend to different conversations in turn or concentrate on one speaker despite the sur-rounding babble. Whether the muscles within the ear play a part in filtering out unwanted sounds during such selective listening has not been established. The less-favourable aspect of the cocktail party effect is that such background noises mask dialogue, making it difficult for persons with sensorineural impairment, such as many elderly individuals, to follow a conversation. In such a situation a single hearing aid may be of little use, but one in each ear may be of more help.

THE PHYSIOLOGY OF BALANCE

The vestibular system is the sensory apparatus of the inner ear that helps the body maintain its postural equi-librium. The information furnished by the vestibular

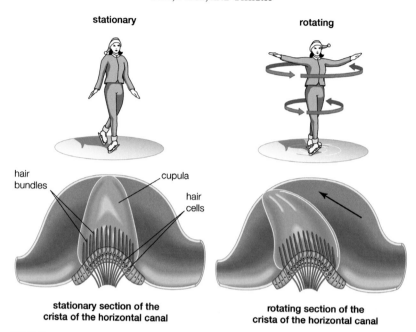

stationary

rotating

hair bundles

cupula

hair cells

stationary section of the
crista of the horizontal canal

rotating section of the
crista of the horizontal canal

In vertebrates the utricular maculae in the inner ear contain an otolithic membrane and otoconia (particles of calcium carbonate) that bend hair cells in the direction of gravity. This response to gravitational pull helps animals maintain their sense of balance. Encyclopædia Britannica, Inc.

system is also essential for coordinating the position of the head and the movement of the eyes. There are two sets of end organs in the inner ear, or labyrinth: the semicircular canals, which respond to rotational movements (angular acceleration); and the utricle and saccule within the vestibule, which respond to changes in the position of the head with respect to gravity (linear acceleration). The information these organs deliver is proprioceptive in character, dealing with events within the body itself, rather than exteroceptive, dealing with events outside the body, as in the case of the responses of the cochlea to sound. Functionally these organs are closely related to the cerebellum and to the reflex

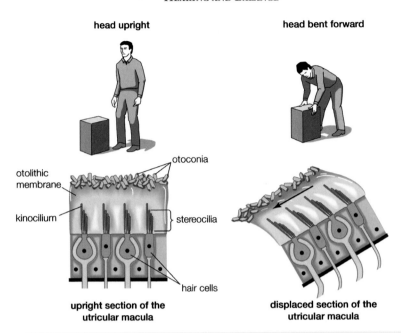

head upright   head bent forward

otoconia

otolithic membrane

kinocilium

stereocilia

hair cells

upright section of the utricular macula

displaced section of the utricular macula

The cristae of the semicircular ducts, which form one of the two sensory organs of balance (the second being the maculae of the utricle and saccule), respond to rotational movements and are involved in dynamic equilibrium. Copyright Encyclopædia Britannica, Inc.; rendering for this edition by Rosen Educational Services

centres of the spinal cord and brainstem that govern the movements of the eyes, neck, and limbs.

Although the vestibular organs and the cochlea are derived embryologically from the same formation, the otic vesicle, their association in the inner ear seems to be a matter more of convenience than of necessity. From both the developmental and the structural point of view, the kinship of the vestibular organs with the lateral line system of the fish is readily apparent. The lateral line system is made up of a series of small sense organs located in the skin of the head and along the sides of the body of fishes. Each organ contains a crista, sensory hair cells, and a cupula, as found in the ampullae of the semicircular ducts. The cristae respond to waterborne vibrations and to pressure changes.

The anatomists of the 17th and 18th centuries assumed that the entire inner ear, including the vestibular apparatus, is devoted to hearing. They were impressed by the orientation of the semicircular canals, which lie in three planes more or less perpendicular to one another, and believed that the canals must be designed for localizing a source of sound in space. The first investigator to present evidence that the vestibular labyrinth is the organ of equilibrium was a French experimental neurologist, Marie-Jean-Pierre Flourens, who in 1824 reported a series of experiments in which he had observed abnormal head movements in pigeons after he had cut each of the semicircular canals in turn. The plane of the movements was always the same as that of the injured canal. Hearing was not affected when he cut the nerve fibres to these organs, but it was abolished when he cut those to the basilar papilla (the bird's uncoiled cochlea). It was not until almost half a century later that the significance of his findings was appreciated and the semicircular canals were recognized as sense organs specifically concerned with the movements and position of the head.

DETECTION OF ANGULAR ACCELERATION: DYNAMIC EQUILIBRIUM

Because the three semicircular canals—superior, posterior, and horizontal—are positioned at right angles to one another, they are able to detect movements in three-dimensional space. When the head begins to rotate in any direction, the inertia of the endolymph causes it to lag behind, exerting pressure that deflects the cupula in the opposite direction. This deflection stimulates the hair cells by bending their stereocilia in the opposite direction.

German physiologist Friedrich Goltz formulated the "hydrostatic concept" in 1870 to explain the working of the semicircular canals. He postulated that the canals are stimulated by the weight of the fluid they contain, the pressure it exerts varying with the head position. In 1873 Austrian scientists Ernst Mach and Josef Breuer and Scottish chemist Crum Brown, working independently, proposed the "hydrodynamic concept," which held that head movements cause a flow of endolymph in the canals and that the canals are then stimulated by the fluid movements or pressure changes. German physiologist J.R. Ewald showed that the compression of the horizontal canal in a pigeon by a small pneumatic hammer causes endolymph movement toward the crista and turning of the head and eyes toward the opposite side. Decompression reverses both the direction of endolymph movement and the turning of the head and eyes. The hydrodynamic concept was proved correct by later investigators who followed the path of a droplet of oil that was injected into the semicircular canal of a live fish. At the start of rotation in the plane of the canal the cupula was deflected in the direction opposite to that of the movement and then returned slowly to its resting position. At the end of rotation it was deflected again, this time in the same direction as the rotation, and then returned once more to its upright stationary position. These deflections resulted from the inertia of the endolymph, which lags behind at the start of rotation and continues its motion after the head has ceased to rotate. The slow return is a function of the elasticity of the cupula itself.

These opposing deflections of the cupula affect the vestibular nerve in different ways, which have been demonstrated in experiments involving the labyrinth removed from a cartilaginous fish. The labyrinth, which remained active for some time after its removal from the animal, was used to record vestibular nerve impulses arising from one of the ampullar cristae. When the labyrinth was at rest there was a slow, continuous, spontaneous discharge of nerve impulses, which was increased by rotation in one direction and decreased by rotation in the other. In other words, the level of excitation rose or fell depending on the direction of rotation.

The deflection of the cupula excites the hair cells by bending the cilia atop them: deflection in one direction depolarizes the cells, whereas deflection in the other direction hyperpolarizes them. Electron-microscopic studies have shown how this polarization occurs. The hair bundles in the cristae are oriented along the axis of each canal. For example, each hair cell of the horizontal canals has its kinocilium facing toward the utricle, whereas each hair cell of the superior canals has its kino-cilium facing away from the utricle. In the horizontal canals deflection of the cupula toward the utricle—i.e., bending of the stereocilia toward the kinocilium—depolarizes the hair cells and increases the rate of discharge. Deflection away from the utricle causes hyper-polarization and decreases the rate of discharge. In superior canals these effects are reversed.

DETECTION OF LINEAR ACCELERATION: STATIC EQUILIBRIUM

The gravity receptors that respond to linear acceleration of the head are the maculae of the utricle and saccule. The left and right utricular maculae are in the same, approxi-mately horizontal, plane and because of this position are more useful in providing information about the position of the head and its side-to-side tilts when a person is in an upright position. The saccular maculae are in parallel vertical planes and probably respond more to forward and backward tilts of the head.

Both pairs of maculae are stimulated by shearing forces between the otolithic membrane and the cilia of the hair cells beneath it. The otolithic membrane is covered with a mass of minute crystals of calcite (otoconia), which add to the membrane's weight and increase the shearing forces set up in response to a slight displacement when the head is tilted. The hair bundles of the macular hair cells are arranged in a particular pattern—facing toward (in the utricle) or away from (in the saccule) a curving midline—that allows detection of all possible head positions. These sensory organs, particularly the utricle, have an important role in the righting reflexes and in reflex control of the muscles of the legs, trunk, and neck that keep the body in an upright position. The role of the saccule is less completely understood. Some investigators have suggested that it is responsive to vibration as well as to linear acceleration of the head in the sagittal (fore and aft) plane. Of the two receptors, the utricle appears to be the dominant partner.

DISTURBANCES OF THE VESTIBULAR SYSTEM

The relation between the vestibular apparatus of the two ears is reciprocal. When the head is turned to the left, the discharge from the left horizontal canal is decreased, and vice versa. Normal posture is the result of their acting in cooperation and in opposition. When the vestibular system of one ear is damaged, the unrestrained activity of the other causes a continuous false sense of turning (vertigo) and rhythmical, jerky movements of the eyes (nystagmus), both toward the uninjured side. When the vestibular hair cells of both inner ears are injured or destroyed, as can occur during treatment with the antibiotics gentamicin or streptomycin, there may be a serious disturbance of posture and gait (ataxia) as well as severe vertigo and disorientation. In younger persons the disturbance tends to subside as reliance is placed on vision and on proprioceptive impulses from the muscles and joints as well as on cutaneous impulses from the soles of the feet to compensate for the loss of information from the semicircular canals. Recovery of some injured hair cells may occur.

Routine tests of vestibular function traditionally have involved stimulation of the semicircular canals to elicit nystagmus and other vestibular ocular reflexes. Rotation, which can cause vertigo and nystagmus, as well as temporary disorientation and a tendency to fall, stimulates the vestibular apparatus of both ears simultaneously. Because otoneurologists are usually more interested in examining the right and left ears separately, they usually employ temperature change as a stimulant. Syringing the ear canal with warm water at 44 °C (111 °F) or with cool water at 30 °C (86 °F) elicits nystagmus by setting up convection currents in the horizontal canal. The duration of the nystagmus may be timed with a stopwatch, or the rate and amplitude of the movements of the eyes can be accurately recorded by picking up the resulting rhythmical variations in the corneoretinal direct current potentials, using electrodes pasted to the skin of the temples—a diagnostic process called electronystagmography. An abnormal vestibular apparatus usually yields a reduced response or no response at all.

The vestibular system may react to unaccustomed stimulation from the motion of an aircraft, ship, or land vehicle to produce a sense of unsteadiness, abdominal discomfort, nausea, and vomiting. Effects not unlike motion sickness, with vertigo and nystagmus, can be observed in the later stages of acute alcoholic intoxication. Vertigo accompanied by hearing loss is a prominent feature of the periodic attacks experienced by patients with Ménière disease, which, until the late 19th century, was confused with epilepsy. It was referred to as apoplectiform cerebral congestion and was treated by purging and bleeding. Other forms of vertigo may present the otoneurologist with more difficult diagnostic problems. Otoneurology is a medical specialty focusing on the relationship between the ear and the brain.

Since the advent of space exploration, interest in experimental and clinical studies of the vestibular system has greatly increased. Investigators are concerned particularly about its performance when persons are exposed to the microgravity of spaceflight, as compared with the Earth's gravitational field for which it evolved. Investigations include the growing use of centrifuges large enough to rotate human subjects, as well as ingeniously automated tests of postural equilibrium for evaluating the vestibulospinal reflexes. Some astronauts have experienced relatively minor vestibular symptoms on returning from spaceflight. Some of these disturbances have lasted for several days, but none have become permanent.

CHAPTER 3

ANATOMY AND PHYSIOLOGY OF THE NOSE AND THROAT

The nose, throat, and surrounding structures are connected anatomically and together serve a key role in protecting the body against invasion by infectious agents. The nose and throat are part of a complex system of sinuses in the head. While various explanations for the existence of sinus cavities have emerged, their primary function appears to lie in the production and drainage of mucus. Mucus production keeps the nasal passages moist and free of dust and infectious agents. The movement of mucus through the passages is facilitated by cilia, which sweep the mucus through the paranasal sinuses, into the nose, and finally into the throat. However, in addition to this collaborative drainage effort, the nose and throat also perform unique functions, such as the detection of odours, in the case of the nose, and swallowing, in the case of the throat.

STRUCTURES OF THE NOSE AND NASAL CAVITY

The nose is the prominent structure between the eyes that serves as the entrance to the respiratory tract and contains the olfactory organ. It provides air for respiration, serves the sense of smell, conditions the air by filtering, warming, and moistening it, and cleans itself of foreign debris extracted from inhalations. These functions are made possible by the various structural elements of the nose, including the unusual scroll-shaped nasal conchae, which form the upper parts of the nasal cavities.

THE NOSE

The nose has two cavities, separated from one another by a wall of cartilage called the septum. The external openings are known as nares or nostrils. The roof of the mouth and the floor of the nose are formed by the palatine bone, the mouth part of which is commonly called the hard palate. A flap of tissue known as the soft palate extends back into the

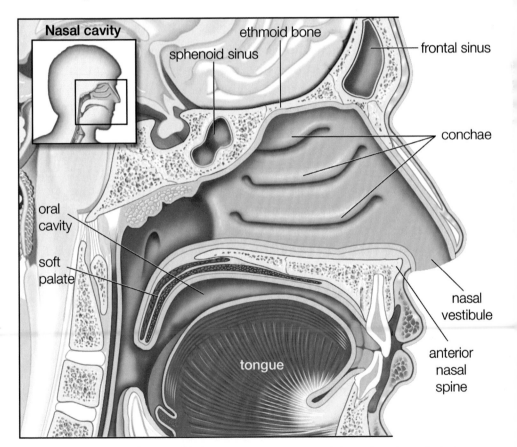

Sagittal (side) view of the human nasal cavity. Encyclopædia Britannica, Inc.

nasopharynx, the nasal portion of the throat, and during swallowing is pressed upward, thus closing off the naso-pharynx so that food is not lodged in the back of the nose.

The shape of the nasal cavity is complex. The forward section, within and above each nostril, is called the vesti-bule. Behind the vestibule and along each outer wall are three elevations, running generally from front to rear. Each elevation, called a nasal concha or turbinate, hangs over an air passage. Beside and above the uppermost con-cha is the olfactory region of the nasal cavity. The rest of the cavity is the respiratory portion. The respiratory area is lined with a moist mucous membrane with fine hairlike projections known as cilia, which serve to collect debris. Mucus from cells in the membrane wall also helps to trap particles of dust, carbon, soot, and bacteria. Sinus cavities are located in the bony skull on both sides of the nose.

In the olfactory (smelling) portion of the nose, most of the lining is mucous membrane. A small segment of the lining contains the nerve cells that are the actual sensory organs. Fibres, called dendrites, which project from the nerve cells into the nasal cavity, are covered only by a thin layer of moisture. The moisture dissolves microscopic particles that the air has carried into the nose from odour-emitting substances, and the particles dissolved in the fluid stimulate the olfactory nerve cells chemically.

NASAL CONCHA

The nasal conchae (singular, nasal concha), or turbi-nates, are thin, scroll-shaped bony elements forming the upper chambers of the nasal cavities. They increase the surface area of these cavities, thus providing for rapid warming and humidification of air as it passes to the lungs. In higher vertebrates the olfactory epithelium is associated with these upper chambers, resulting in keener sense of smell. In humans, who are less dependent on the sense of smell, the nasal conchae are much reduced. The components of the nasal conchae are known as the inferior, medial, superior, and supreme turbinates.

PARANASAL AIR SINUSES

The air sinuses, four on each side, are cavities in the bones that adjoin the nose. They are outgrowths from the nasal cavity and retain their communications with it by means of drainage openings, or ostia. Consequently, their lining is mucous membrane similar to that found in the nose. The mucus secretion formed is propelled by cilia through the ostia of the sinuses to the nasal cavity. From there it is eventually swallowed or expelled. All sinuses are absent or small at birth, and they gradually enlarge until puberty, when they usually grow rapidly.

The two frontal sinuses are situated in the frontal bone immediately above and between the eye sockets, or orbits. They are usually unequal in size and have the shape of an irregular pyramid with its apex directed upward. The thin bony wall separating the two cavities sometimes is absent.

It is rare to recognize the frontal sinuses until the age of seven years, and their maximum growth occurs after puberty. They vary considerably in size and are usually larger in the male than in the female, averaging, when fully developed, approximately 3 cm (1.2 inches) in height, 2.5 cm (1 inch) in width, and 2 cm (0.8 inch) in depth. The front, or anterior, wall is thick skull bone. Behind the sinuses lies bone covering the brain, and the floor of the sinuses slopes toward their openings into the nose.

The maxillary sinuses are not only the largest of the air sinuses but also the first to appear, being present in the fourth month of intrauterine life. Each is a pyramidal space, its roof formed by the floor of the eye socket, and its floor by the palate and teeth-bearing bone. The roots of the upper-jaw teeth may project through the floor into the sinus cavity or may be so closely related to the floor that extraction leads to the formation of an opening between mouth and sinus (oro-antral fistula). The maxillary sinuses reach their maximum size by about age 12, when all the permanent teeth except the third molars have erupted. The nerves supplying the upper teeth run through the front wall of the sinus and may be irritated during acute antral infections with resultant toothache.

The ethmoidal sinuses, from 3 to 18 thin-walled cavities between the nasal cavities and the eye sockets, make up the ethmoidal labyrinths. Their walls form most of the inner walls of the eye sockets and are joined together by a thin perforated plate of bone at the roof of the nose. This bone, the cribriform plate, transmits the olfactory nerves that carry the sense of smell.

The sinuses contained within each labyrinth are arranged in three noncommunicating groups, all of which open into the nasal cavity. All produce mucus whose function is to lubricate the cilia lining the nasal passages.

The sphenoidal sinuses are situated in the back of the nose in the sphenoidal bone, which forms a forward part of the base of the skull and contains the depression, or fossa, for the pituitary gland. The sinuses are separated from each other by a bony wall, or septum, that is rarely in the midline, and they discharge their mucus through an opening in the front wall of the sinus into the nose.

These sinuses appear before birth but remain small until the age of 10, when they grow rapidly. Rapid growth also occurs at about puberty. Sphenoidal sinuses are important in the surgical approach to the pituitary gland for patients with breast cancer or pituitary tumours.

Comprehensive studies on the comparative anatomy and physiology of the nose and paranasal sinuses have been made in humans and in lower animals. The presence of the sphenoidal and frontal sinuses in carnivores such as the dog, hyena, and tiger is related to an increased area of olfaction and consequent improvement in the sense of smell. Ethmoidal air cells are found only in higher apes and humans and are probably the result of restriction of the olfactory area.

The maxillary sinuses are largest in humans, in the higher apes, and in capuchin and howler monkeys and are absent in baboons, lorises, and tapirs. It has been suggested that the maxillary sinuses play a part in phonation (vocalization), that they aid in conservation of heat from the nasal fossae, and that they serve to lighten the skull, but evidence for these theories is lacking.

PALATE

The palate forms the roof of the mouth and separates the oral and nasal cavities. It consists of an anterior hard palate of bone and, in mammals, a posterior soft palate that has no skeletal support and terminates in a fleshy, elongated projection called the uvula.

The hard palate, which composes two-thirds of the total palate area, is a plate of bone covered by a moist, durable layer of mucous-membrane tissue, which secretes small amounts of mucus. This layer forms several ridges that help grip food while the tongue agitates it during chewing. The hard palate provides space for the tongue to move freely and supplies a rigid floor to the nasal cavity so that pressures within the mouth do not close off the nasal passage.

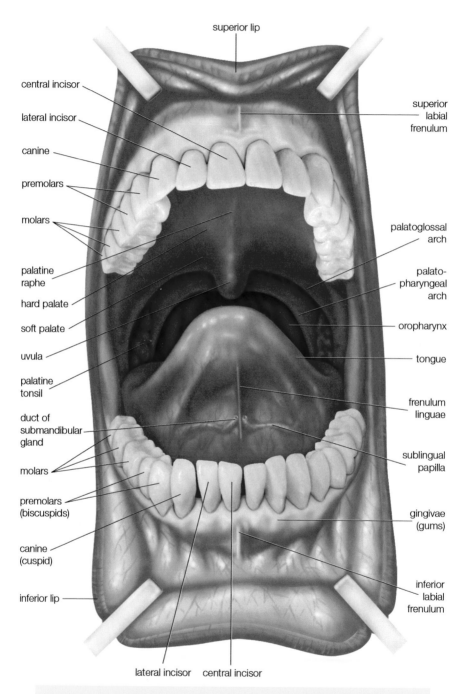

superior lip

central incisor

lateral incisor

canine

premolars

molars

palatine raphe

hard palate

soft palate

uvula

palatine tonsil

duct of submandibular gland

molars

premolars (biscuspids)

canine (cuspid)

inferior lip

superior labial frenulum

palatoglossal arch

palato- pharyngeal arch

oropharynx

tongue

frenulum linguae

sublingual papilla

gingivae (gums)

inferior labial frenulum

lateral incisor   central incisor

Anterior view of the oral cavity. Encyclopædia Britannica, Inc.

The soft palate is composed of muscle and connective tissue, which give it both mobility and support. This palate is very flexible. When elevated for swallowing and sucking, it completely blocks and separates the nasal cavity and nasal portion of the pharynx from the mouth and the oral part of the pharynx. While elevated, the soft palate creates a vacuum in the oral cavity, which keeps food out of the respiratory tract.

The first well-developed palates are found in the reptiles, although only in the form of a hard partition. Palates similar to those in humans occur only in birds and some mammals. In a few whales the mucous membrane forms toughened plates known as baleen, or whalebone.

THE THROAT AND ASSOCIATED STRUCTURES

The pharynx, which is Greek for "throat," is a cone-shaped passageway leading from the oral and nasal cavities in the head to the esophagus and larynx, or voice box. The pharynx chamber serves both respiratory and digestive functions. Thick fibres of muscle and connective tissue attach the pharynx to the base of the skull and surrounding structures. Both circular and longitudinal muscles occur in the walls of this organ. The circular muscles form constrictions that help push food to the esophagus and prevent air from being swallowed, while the longitudinal fibres lift the walls of the pharynx during swallowing.

PHARYNX

The pharynx consists of three main divisions. The anterior portion is the nasal pharynx, the back section of the nasal cavity. The nasal pharynx connects to the second

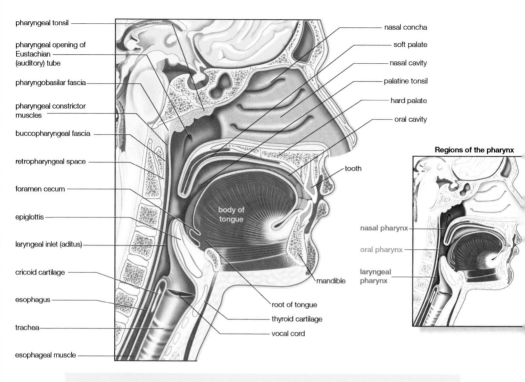

Sagittal (side) section of the pharynx. Encyclopædia Britannica, Inc.

region, the oral pharynx, by means of a passage called an isthmus. The oral pharynx begins at the back of the mouth cavity and continues down the throat to the epiglottis, a flap of tissue that covers the air passage to the lungs and that channels food to the esophagus. Triangular-shaped recesses in the walls of this region house the palatine tonsils, two masses of lymphatic tissue prone to infection. The isthmus connecting the oral and nasal regions is extremely beneficial in humans. It allows them to breathe through either the nose or the mouth and, when medically necessary, allows food to be passed to the esophagus by nasal tubes. The third region is the laryngeal pharynx, which begins at the epiglottis and leads down to the esophagus. Its function is to regulate the passage of air to the lungs and food to the esophagus.

Two small tubes (eustachian tubes) connect the middle ears to the pharynx and allow air pressure on the eardrum to be equalized. Head colds sometimes inflame these tubes, causing earaches and hearing difficulties. Other medical afflictions associated with the pharynx include tonsillitis, cancer, and various types of throat paralyses caused by polio, diphtheria, rabies, or nervous-system injuries.

Larynx

The larynx, or voice box, is a hollow, tubular structure that is connected to the top of the windpipe (trachea). Air passes through the larynx on its way to the lungs. The larynx also produces vocal sounds and prevents the passage of food and other foreign particles into the lower respiratory tracts.

The larynx is composed of an external skeleton of cartilage plates that prevents collapse of the structure. The plates are fastened together by membranes and muscle fibres. The front set of plates, called thyroid cartilage, has a central ridge and elevation commonly known as the Adam's apple. The plates tend to be replaced by bone cells beginning from about 20 years of age onward.

The epiglottis, at the upper part of the larynx, is a flap-like projection into the throat. As food is swallowed, the whole larynx structure rises to the epiglottis so that the passageway to the respiratory tract is blocked. After the food passes into the esophagus (food tube), the larynx relaxes and resumes its natural position.

The centre portion of the larynx is reduced to slitlike openings in two sites. Both sites represent large folds in the mucous membrane lining the larynx. The first pair is known as the false vocal cords, while the second is the true vocal cords (glottis). Muscles attached directly and indirectly to

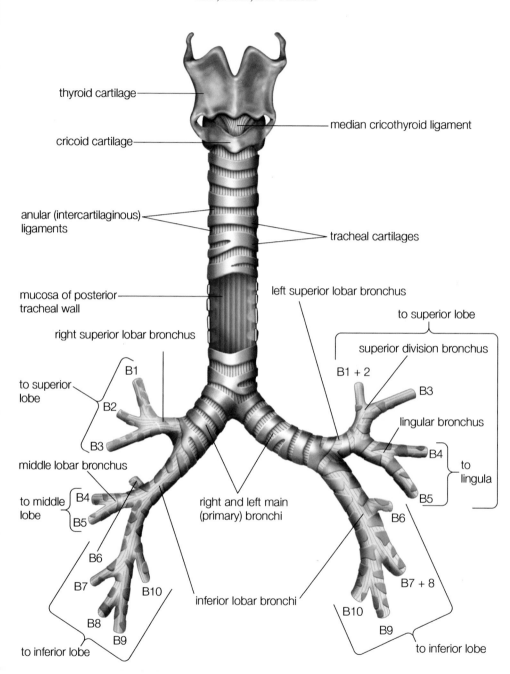

The trachea and major bronchi of the human lungs. Encyclopædia Britannica, Inc.

the vocal cords permit the opening and closing of the folds. Speech is normally produced when air expelled from the lungs moves up the trachea and strikes the underside of the vocal cords, setting up vibrations as it passes through them. Raw sound emerges from the larynx and passes to the upper cavities, which act as resonating chambers (or in some languages, such as Arabic, as shapers of sound), and then passes through the mouth for articulation by the tongue, teeth, hard and soft palates, and lips. If the larynx is removed, the esophagus can function as the source for sound, but the control of pitch and volume is lacking.

In other forms of animal life, sounds can be produced by the glottis, but in most, the ability to form words is lacking. Reptiles can produce a hissing sound by rushing air through the glottis, which is at the back of the mouth. Frogs produce their croaking sounds by passing air back and forth over the vocal folds; a pair of vocal sacs near the mouth serve as resonating chambers. In birds the larynx is a small structure in front of the trachea; it serves only to guard the air passage.

Vocal Cords

The vocal cords (Latin: *plica vocalis*) are two folds of mucous membrane that extend across the interior cavity of the larynx and are primarily responsible for voice production. Sound is produced by the vibration of the folds in response to the passage between them of air exhaled from the lungs. The frequency of these vibrations determines the pitch of the voice. The vocal cords are shorter and thinner in women and children, accounting in part for their higher-pitched voices.

The ventricular folds, located just above the vocal cords, are sometimes called false vocal cords because they are not involved in voice production.

Tonsils

The tonsils are small masses of lymphatic tissue located in the wall of the pharynx at the rear of the throat. In humans the term *tonsil* is used to designate any of three sets of tonsils, most commonly the palatine tonsils (the other two sets are known as the adenoids, or pharyngeal tonsils, and the lingual tonsils). The palatine tonsils are a pair of oval-shaped masses protruding from each side of the oral pharynx behind the mouth cavity. The exposed surface of each tonsil is marked by numerous pits that lead to deeper lymphatic tissue. Debris frequently lodges in the pits and causes inflammation, a condition called tonsillitis. The function of the palatine tonsils is thought to be associated with preventing infection in the respiratory and digestive tracts by producing antibodies that help kill infective agents. Frequently, however, the tonsils themselves become the objects of infection, and surgical removal (tonsillectomy) is required. Usually, children are more prone to tonsillitis than adults, for the structures tend to degenerate and decrease in size as one gets older.

The lingual tonsils are aggregations of lymphatic tissue on the surface tissue at the base of the tongue. The surface of this tonsil has pits leading to lower lymphatic tissue as in the other two tonsil types, but these pits are effectively drained by small glands (mucous glands), and infection is rare.

Adenoids

The adenoids, or pharyngeal tonsils, are masses of lymphatic tissue, similar to the (palatine) tonsils, that is attached to the back wall of the nasal pharynx (i.e., the upper part of the throat opening into the nasal cavity

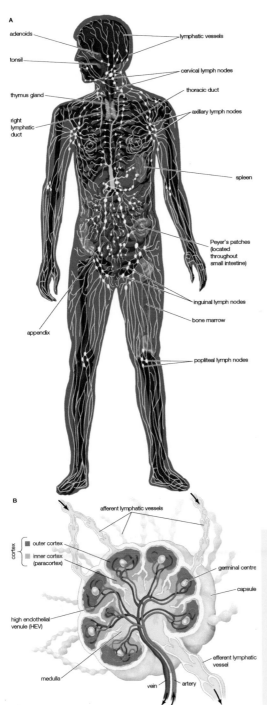

A

adenoids
tonsil
thymus gland
right lymphatic duct
appendix

lymphatic vessels
cervical lymph nodes
thoracic duct
axillary lymph nodes
spleen
Peyer's patches (located throughout small intestine)
inguinal lymph nodes
bone marrow
popliteal lymph nodes

B

afferent lymphatic vessels

cortex
  outer cortex
  inner cortex (paracortex)

germinal centre
capsule

high endothelial venule (HEV)

medulla

efferent lymphatic vessel

vein   artery

A. The human lymphatic system, showing the lymphatic vessels and lymphoid organs. B. Internal and external structures of a lymph node. Encyclopædia Britannica, Inc.

proper). An individual fold of such nasopharyngeal lymphatic tissue is called an adenoid.

The surface layer of the adenoids consists of ciliated epithelial cells covered by a thin film of mucus. The cilia move constantly in a wavelike manner and propel the blanket of mucus down to the pharynx proper. From that point the mucus is caught by the swallowing action of the pharyngeal (throat) muscles and is sent down to the stomach. The adenoids also contain glands that secrete mucus to replenish the surface film. The function of the adenoids is protective. The moving film of mucus tends to carry infectious agents and dust particles

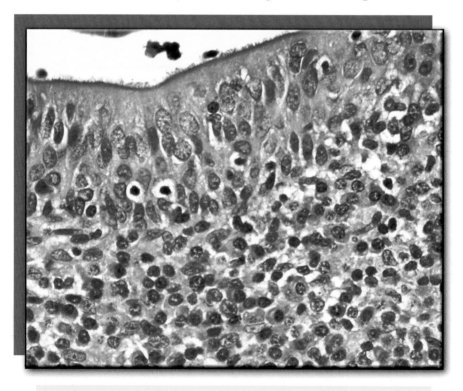

The surface layer of adenoid tissue consists of ciliated epithelial cells. The cilia project from the cell surface into the pharynx (the large white space visible at the top). Photo courtesy of Laura P. Hale, M.D., Ph.D., Duke University Medical Center

inhaled through the nose down to the pharynx, where the epithelium is more resistant. Immune substances, or antibodies, are thought to be formed within the lymphatic tissue, which, combined with phagocytic action, tends to arrest and absorb infectious agents.

The adenoids usually enlarge in early childhood. Infections in childhood can cause swelling and inflammation of the adenoids and may permanently enlarge them. Large adenoids obstruct breathing through the nose and interfere with sinus drainage, thus predisposing the person to infections of the sinuses. Chronic respiratory obstruction and the resultant mouth breathing produce a characteristic vacant facial expression on a person with enlarged adenoids. The adenoids' infection and enlargement also predispose to blockage of the eustachian tubes (the passages extending from the nasal pharynx to the middle ear) and thus to middle-ear infections. Surgical removal, often in conjunction with the removal of the tonsils, is frequently recommended for children with enlarged or infected adenoids. Adenoids normally decrease in size after childhood.

THE PHYSIOLOGY OF TASTE AND SMELL

Specialized tissues in the nose and oral cavity are responsible for producing the sensations of taste and smell. Taste (gustation) is made possible by taste receptor cells that are aggregated into structures known as taste buds, different types of which are distributed across the tongue. Smell (olfaction) is made possible by a unique membrane found in the nose that contains hair cells capable of trapping odour molecules. The senses of taste and smell combine to produce the perceived attribute of flavour.

TASTE SENSE

The sensory structures for taste are the taste buds, clusters of cells contained in goblet-shaped structures called papillae that open by a small pore to the mouth cavity. The cells of taste buds, which are known as taste receptor cells and with which incoming chemicals from food and other sources interact, occur on the tongue in groups of 50–150. Each of these groups forms a taste bud, which itself is grouped together with other taste buds to form taste papillae. Taste buds are located primarily in fungiform (mushroom-shaped), foliate, and circumvallate (walled-around) papillae of the tongue or in adjacent structures of the palate and throat.

The taste buds make contact with the outside environment through a taste pore. Slender processes (microvilli) extend from the outer ends of the receptor cells through the taste pore, where the processes are covered by the mucus that lines the oral cavity. At their inner ends the taste receptor cells synapse, or connect, with afferent sensory neurons, nerve cells that conduct information to the brain. Each receptor cell synapses with several afferent sensory neurons, and each afferent neuron branches to several taste papillae, where each branch makes contact with many receptor cells. The afferent sensory neurons occur in three different nerves running to the brain—the facial nerve, the glossopharyngeal nerve, and the vagus nerve.

Taste receptor cells, which differentiate from the surrounding epithelium, are replaced by new cells in a turnover period as short as 7 to 10 days. The various types of cells in the taste bud appear to be different stages in this turnover process.

On average, the human tongue has 2,000–8,000 taste buds, implying that there are hundreds of thousands of

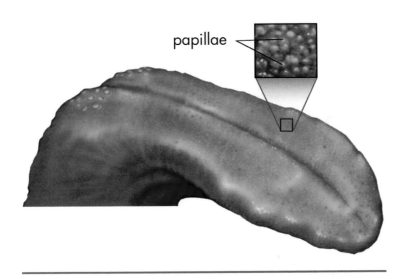

papillae

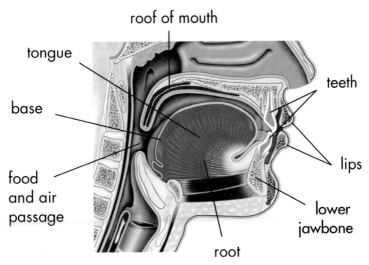

roof of mouth

tongue

base

food
and air
passage

teeth

lips

lower
jawbone

root

Taste buds on the human tongue exhibit sensitivity to specific tastes.
Encyclopædia Britannica, Inc.

receptor cells. However, the number of taste buds varies widely. For example, per square centimetre on the tip of the tongue, some people may have only a few individual taste buds, whereas others may have more than one thousand. This variability contributes to differences in the taste sensations experienced by different people. Taste sensations produced within an individual taste bud also vary, since each taste bud typically contains receptor cells that respond to distinct chemical stimuli—as opposed to the same chemical stimulus. As a result, the sensation of different tastes (i.e., salty, sweet, sour, bitter, or umami) is diverse not only within a single taste bud but also throughout the surface of the tongue.

Many gustatory receptors in small papillae on the soft palate and back roof of the mouth in adults are particularly sensitive to sour and bitter tastes, whereas the tongue receptors are relatively more sensitive to sweet and salty tastes. Some loss of taste sensitivity suffered among denture wearers may occur because of mechanical interference of the dentures with taste receptors on the roof of the mouth.

NERVE SUPPLY

There is no single sensory nerve for taste. The anterior (front) two-thirds of the tongue is supplied by one nerve (the lingual nerve), the back of the tongue by another (the glossopharyngeal nerve), and the throat and larynx by certain branches of a third (the vagus nerve), all of which subserve touch, temperature, and pain sensitivity in the tongue, as well as taste. The gustatory fibres of the anterior tongue leave the lingual nerve to form the chorda tympani, a slender nerve that traverses the eardrum on the way to the brainstem. When the chorda tympani at one ear is cut or damaged (by injury to the eardrum), taste buds begin to disappear and gustatory sensitivity is lost on the anterior two-thirds of the tongue on the same side. The taste fibres from all the sensory nerves from the mouth come together in the medulla oblongata. Here and at all levels of the brain, gustatory fibres run in distinct and separate pathways, lying close to the pathways for other modalities from the tongue and mouth cavity. From the medulla, the gustatory fibres ascend by a pathway to a small cluster of cells in the thalamus and then to a taste-receiving area in the anterior cerebral cortex.

PHYSIOLOGICAL BASIS OF TASTE

No simple relationship has been found between the chemical composition of stimuli and the quality of gustatory experience except in the case of acids. The taste qualities of inorganic salts (such as potassium bromide) are complex. For example, epsom salt (magnesium sulfate) is commonly sensed as bitter, while table salt (sodium chloride) is typical of sodium salts, which usually yield the familiar saline taste. Sweet and bitter tastes are elicited by many different classes of chemical compound.

Theorists of taste sensitivity classically posited only four basic or primary types of human taste receptors, one for each gustatory quality: salty, sour, bitter, and sweet. Yet, recordings of sensory impulses in the taste nerves of laboratory animals show that many individual nerve fibres from the tongue are of mixed sensitivity, responding to more than one of the basic taste stimuli, such as acid plus salt or acid plus salt plus sugar. Other individual nerve fibres respond to stimuli of only one basic gustatory quality. Most numerous, however, are taste fibres subserving two basic taste sensitivities; those subserving one or three qualities are about equal in number and next most frequent; fibres that respond to all four primary stimuli are least common. Mixed sensitivity may be only partly attributed to multiple branches of taste nerve endings. In humans, tastes of sugars, synthetic sweeteners, weak salt solutions, and some unpleasant medications are blocked by gymnemic acid, a drug obtained from *Gymnema* bushes native to India. Among some laboratory animals, gymnemic acid blocks only the nerve response to sugar, even if the fibre mediates other taste qualities. Such a multiresponsive fibre still can transmit taste impulses (e.g., for salt or sour), so that blockage by the drug can be attributed to chemically specific sites or cells in the taste bud.

In some animals (e.g., the cat), specific taste receptors appear to be activated by water. These water receptors are inhibited by weak saline solutions. Water taste might be considered a fifth gustatory quality in addition to the basic four.

THE QUALITIES OF TASTE

The four recognized qualities of taste—sour, salt, sweet, and bitter—have been investigated extensively. Another, more recently recognized quality of taste, known as umami, has raised intriguing questions about taste sensation and the characteristics of the chemicals that are distinguished by taste buds.

Sour

The hydrogen ions of acids (e.g., hydrochloric acid) are largely responsible for the sour taste. However, although a stimulus grows more sour as its hydrogen ion (H^+) concentration increases, this factor alone does not determine sourness. Weak organic acids (e.g., the acetic acid in vinegar) taste more sour than would be predicted from their hydrogen ion concentration alone. Hence, it appears that the rest of the acid molecule affects the efficiency with which hydrogen ions stimulate.

Contestants munch on sour pickles at the sixth annual pickle eating competition at the Carnegie Deli in New York, New York, on May 19, 2004. New York Daily News Archive/Getty Images

Salt

Although saltiness is often associated with water-soluble salts, most such compounds (except sodium chloride) have complex tastes such as bitter-salt or sour-salt. Salts of low molecular weight are predominantly salty, while those of higher molecular weight tend to be bitter. The salts of heavy metals such as mercury have a metallic taste, although some of the salts of lead (especially lead acetate) and beryllium are sweet. Both parts of the molecule (e.g., lead and acetate) contribute to taste quality and to stimulating efficiency. The following is a series for degree of saltiness, in decreasing order: ammonium (most salty), potassium, calcium, sodium, lithium, and magnesium salts (least salty).

Sweet

Except for some salts of lead or beryllium, sweetness is associated largely with organic compounds (such as alcohols, glycols, sugars, and sugar derivatives). Sensitivity to synthetic sweeteners (e.g., saccharin) is especially remarkable; the taste of saccharin can be detected in a dilution 700 times weaker than that required for cane sugar. The stereochemical (spatial) arrangement of atoms within a molecule may affect its taste. Thus, slight changes within a sweet molecule will make it bitter or tasteless.

Several theorists have proposed that the common feature for all of the sweet stimuli is the presence in the molecule of a proton acceptor, such as the OH (hydroxyl) components of carbohydrates (e.g., sugars) and many other sweet-tasting compounds. It has also been theorized that such molecules will not taste sweet unless they are of appropriate size.

Bitter

The experience of a bitter taste is elicited by many classes of chemical compounds and often is associated with sweet

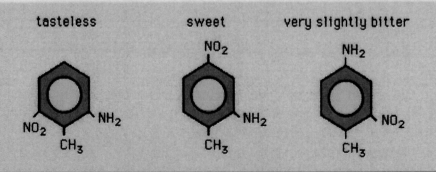

Effects of molecular arrangement on taste sensation. Copyright Encyclopædia Britannica, Inc.; rendering for this edition by Rosen Educational Services

and other gustatory qualities. Among bitter substances are such alkaloids (often toxic) as quinine, caffeine, and strychnine. Most of these substances have extremely low taste thresholds and are detectable in very weak concentrations. The size of such molecules is theoretically held to account for whether or not they will taste bitter. An increase in molecular weight of inorganic salts or an increase in length of chains of carbonw atoms in organic molecules tends to be associated with increased bitterness.

A substantial minority of people exhibit specific taste blindness, an inability to detect as bitter such chemicals as phenylthiocarbamide (PTC). Taste blindness for PTC and other carbamides appears to be hereditary (as a recessive trait), occurring in about a third of Europeans and in roughly 40 percent of the people in Western India. Taste blindness for carbamides is not correlated with insensitivity to other bitter stimuli.

Umami

Umami is often considered the fifth basic taste because it is distinctly different from the other basic tastes, and it is believed to activate a separate set of taste receptors. Umami was identified as the rich flavour imparted by the amino acid L-glutamate in seaweed. Monosodium glutamate (MSG) became the first umami flavour enhancer to be used commercially.

FLAVOUR

Flavour (or flavor) is an attribute of a substance that is produced by a combination of the senses of smell, taste, and touch and is perceived within the mouth.

Tasting occurs chiefly on the tongue through the taste buds. Substances can be tasted only when they are in water solutions, and if a substance is not in solution when taken into the mouth, it must be dissolved in saliva before it can be detected by the taste buds.

The sense of smell involves the olfactory nerve endings in the upper part of the interior of the nose. Aromas can reach these nerves either directly through the nostrils, as in breathing, or indirectly up the back passageway from the mouth. Because of their remote location, the olfactory nerve endings are best stimulated by inhaling through the nose or swallowing if food is in the mouth. Odours are detected only when the material is in gaseous form—i.e., a dispersion of molecules in air. Disorders of smell greatly affect the ability to detect flavours.

Touch sensations that contribute to taste originate in the nose, on the lips, and throughout the entire mouth and throat. The touch sensations relating solely to flavour are based on the chemical properties of the substance. Reactions induced by chemical properties include the coolness of peppermint, the "bite" of mustard and pepper, and the warmth of cloves.

When a person consumes food, the simultaneous stimulation of the senses of taste, smell, and touch creates an immediate impression that causes the individual to accept the food and continue eating it or to reject it. Many foods such as bananas, berries, and other fruits, nuts, milk, and a few vegetables have flavours that make them highly acceptable in their natural, uncooked state. Other foods derive their flavour through cooking, seasoning, and flavouring or combinations of these. Preference for or avoidance of a particular flavour is generally a learned behaviour.

FACTORS AFFECTING TASTE SENSITIVITY

Fluids of extreme temperature, especially those that are cold, may produce temporary taste insensitivity. People generally seem to taste most acutely when the stimulus is at or slightly below body temperature. When the tongue and mouth are first adapted to the temperature of a taste solution, sugar sensitivity increases with temperature rise, salt and quinine sensitivity decrease, and acid sensitivity is relatively unchanged. Gustatory adaptation (partial or complete disappearance of taste sensitivity) may occur if a solution is held in the mouth for a period of time. The effect of one adapting stimulus on the sensitivity to another one (cross adaptation) is especially common with substances that are chemically similar and that elicit the same taste quality. Adaptation to sodium chloride will reduce one's ability to sense the saltiness of a variety of the inorganic salts but will leave undiminished or even enhance qualities such as bitterness, sweetness, or sourness that were part of the taste of the salt before adaptation. Likewise, adaptation by one acid may reduce sensitivity to the sourness of other acids.

Adaptation studies often are complicated by so-called contrast effects. For example, people say that distilled water tastes sweet following their exposure to a weak acid. Water may take on other taste qualities as well. For example, following one's adaptation to a sour-bitter chemical such as urea, water may taste salty. Adaptation tends to diminish or enhance the effect of a subsequent stimulus depending on whether the two stimuli normally elicit the same or a contrasting taste. Thus, the adapted sweetness of water and all normally sweet-tasting substances are enhanced after one has tasted acid (sour). The bitterness of tea and coffee or the sourness of lemon are masked or suppressed by sugar or saccharin.

The human gustatory difference threshold (for a just noticeable difference in intensity) is approximately a 20 percent change in concentration. For very weak taste stimuli, however, the threshold sensitivity is less.

FOOD CHOICE

One's ability to taste is intimately involved with his or her eating habits or with his or her rejection of noxious substances. One of the earliest reflex responses of the infant, that of sucking, can be controlled by gustatory stimuli. Sweet solutions are sucked more readily than plain water. In contrast, bitter, salty, or sour stimuli tend to stop the sucking reflex.

Many animals provide clear examples of beneficially selective feeding behaviour. Laboratory rats, when given an unhampered choice of carbohydrates, proteins, vitamins, and minerals (each in a separate container), show consistent patterns of selection that may be modified by physiological stresses and strains. A rat made salt-deficient by removal of its adrenal glands, for example, will increase its intake of sodium chloride sufficiently to maintain health and growth. Normally, such gland removal is fatal in the absence of salt-replacement therapy. Histories of similar effects have been reported in humans, one case being that of a child with an adrenal disorder who kept himself alive by satisfying an intense salt craving.

Among adults, past experience strongly influences eating habits, sometimes to the point that physiological well-being suffers. Food habits and other factors play a significant role in eating behaviour.

Taste alone is not a reliable guide to safety. Poisonous substances often are unpalatable, but not invariably. Lead acetate, sometimes called sugar of lead, once was used as a sweetening agent with disastrous results before its potentially fatal effects were discovered. Many palatable substances, including some synthetic sweeteners, are toxic.

Taste aversions may be established by conditioning, even for substances that have been previously preferred. In one study, a rat tasted saccharin solution three hours before being exposed to enough radiation to become sick. When the animal recovered, it was found to have a strong aversion to the taste of saccharin. Other aversions selectively can be produced by injecting an individual with a nauseating drug before or after a specific taste experience. For example, the medication disulfiram (Antabuse), used in the treatment of alcoholism, reacts with alcohol to produce nausea and vomiting. An unusual finding is that long delays of up to several hours in the time between the presentation of the taste stimulus and the induction of illness do not prevent the conditioning. In most other studies, only brief intervals (perhaps up to minutes in duration) have been found to result in successful conditioning. Positive preferences also are subject to conditioning, as when the tastes of drugs or vitamins become associated with the feelings of well-being they generate.

SMELL SENSE

In humans the olfactory receptors are located high in the nasal cavity. The yellow-pigmented olfactory membrane covers about 2.5 square cm (0.4 square inch) on each side of the inner nose. Olfactory receptors are long thin cells ending in 6 to 12 delicate hairs called cilia that project into and through the mucus that normally covers the nasal epithelium, or lining. The end of each receptor narrows to a fine nerve fibre, which, along with many others, travels through a channel in the bony roof of the nasal cavity and enters either of two specialized structures called olfactory bulbs—stemlike projections under the front part of the brain—to end in a series of intricate basketlike clusters called glomeruli. Each glomerulus receives impulses from about 26,000 receptors and sends them on through other cells, eventually to reach higher olfactory centres at the base of the brain. Fibres also cross from one olfactory bulb to the other.

Odorous molecules are carried to the olfactory region by slight eddies in the air during quiet breathing, but vigorous sniffing brings a surge of air into the olfactory region. Odour sensitivity may be impaired by blocking the nasal passages mechanically, as when membranes are congested by infection.

Pain endings of the trigeminal nerve fibres are widely distributed throughout the nasal cavity, including the olfactory region. Relatively mild odorants, such as orange oil, as well as the more obvious irritants, such as ammonia, stimulate such nerve endings as well as the olfactory receptors.

OLFACTORY QUALITIES

The vocabulary of odour is rich with names of substances that elicit a great variety of olfactory qualities. One of the best-known published psychological attempts at classification was in 1916 on the basis of more than 400 different scents on human subjects. On the basis of the apparent similarities of perceived odour quality or confusions in naming, it was concluded that there were six main odour qualities: fruity, flowery, resinous, spicy, foul, and burned.

Electrical activity can be detected with fine insulated wires inserted into the olfactory bulb. Portions of the olfactory bulb toward the anterior or oral region in the rabbit are found to be more sensitive to water-soluble substances, whereas the more posterior parts of the olfactory bulb are more sensitive to fat-soluble substances. In addition, when very fine electrodes are used, individual cells (mitral cells) are sensitive to different groups of chemicals. Evidence for the existence of only a few primary receptors, however, does not emerge from such studies. Rather, a variety of different combinations of sensitivity has been found. Similarly, recordings from the primary receptor nerve fibres reveal different patterns of sensitivity. Electrical recording of this type also shows that olfactory sensitivity can be enhanced by a painful stimulus, such as a pinch on the foot. This appears to be a reflex that serves to enhance the detection of dangerous stimuli in the environment. Different parts of the olfactory neural pathways seem to be selectively tuned to discriminate different classes of olfactory information. For example, the third- and fourth-order olfactory neurons found beyond the olfactory bulb of the rat seem particularly concerned with distinguishing the odour of sexually receptive females. These neurons appear to be especially important in the preference the male rat shows for the smell of urine from the female in heat.

Odourous Substances

To be odorous, a substance must be sufficiently volatile for its molecules to be given off and carried into the nostrils by air currents. The solubility of the substance also seems to play a role. Chemicals that are soluble in water or fat tend to be strong odorants. No unique chemical or physical property that can be said to elicit the experience of odour has yet been discovered.

Only seven of the chemical elements are odorous: fluorine, chlorine, bromine, iodine, oxygen (as ozone), phosphorus, and arsenic. Most odorous substances are organic (carbon-containing) compounds in which both the arrangement of atoms within the molecule as well as the particular chemical groups that comprise the molecule influence odour. Stereoisomers (i.e., different spatial arrangements of the same molecular components) may have different odours. On the other hand, a series of different molecules that derive from benzene all have a similar odour. It is of historic interest that the first benzene derivatives studied by chemists were found in pleasant-smelling substances from plants (such as oil of wintergreen or oil of anise), and so the entire class of compounds was labelled aromatic. Subsequently, other so-called aromatic compounds were identified that have less-attractive odours.

The scent of flowers and roots (such as ginger) depends upon the presence of minute quantities of highly odorous essential oils. Although the major odour constituents can be identified by chemical analysis, some botanical essences are so complex that their odours can be duplicated only by adding them in small amounts to synthetic formulations.

ODOUR SENSITIVITY

In spite of the relative inaccessibility of the olfactory receptor cells, odour stimuli can be detected at extremely low concentrations. Olfaction is said to be 10,000 times more sensitive than taste. A threshold value for the odorant ethyl mercaptan (found in rotten meat) has been cited in the range of 1/400,000,000th of a milligram per litre of air. A just-noticeable difference in odour intensity may be apparent when there is a 20 percent increase in odorant strength, but at low concentrations as much as a 100 percent increase in concentration may be required.

Temperature influences the strength of an odour by affecting the volatility and therefore the emission of odorous particles from the source. Humidity also affects odour for the same reasons. Hunting dogs can follow a spoor (odour trail) most easily when high humidity retards evaporation and dissipation of the odour. Perfumes contain chemicals called fixatives, added to retard evaporation of the more volatile constituents. The temporary anosmia (absence of sense of smell) following colds may be complete or partial. In the latter case, only the odours of certain substances are affected. Paranosmia (change in perceived odour quality) also may occur during respiratory infections. Changes in sensitivity are reported to occur in women during the menstrual cycle, particularly in regard to certain odorants (steroids) related to sex hormones. Olfactory sensitivity also is said to become more acute during hunger.

Adaptation to odours is so striking that the stench of a junkyard or chemical laboratory ceases to be a nuisance after a few minutes have passed. Olfactory adaptation, as measured by a rise in threshold, is especially pronounced for stronger odours. Cross adaptation (between different odours) may take place. Thus, eucalyptus oil may be difficult to detect after one becomes adapted to the smell of camphor. Adaptation was long regarded solely as the result of changes in the olfactory receptor. However, the receptor cells in the nose seem to adapt only partially. Rhythmic discharges continue in the olfactory bulb long after one ceases to detect an odour. Apparently, some olfactory adaptation may occur in the brain as well as in the sense organ.

EFFECTS ON BEHAVIOUR

Mammals in the wild state appear to utilize their odour glands for sexual attraction. Rats show a preference for the branch of a maze that has been scented with the odour of a sexually receptive female. It is likely that some rudiments of these effects operate in humans. The most sexually provocative perfumes have a high proportion of musk or a musklike odour. Genuine musk is derived from the sexual glands of the musk deer and is chemically related to human sex hormones. As previously mentioned, odour sensitivity in humans varies with the menstrual cycle.

Among laboratory animals the secretion of reproductive hormones can be markedly influenced by odour stimulation. This seems to be an innate physiological process rather than the result of learning. When the odour of a strange male is presented to a recently mated female, pregnancy block occurs. The normal hormonal changes following copulation are blocked under these conditions, and the fertilized egg fails to survive. A related study of the periodicity and length of the menstrual cycle in women exposed to the normal odours of men suggests that there may be similar effects among humans. Human behaviour, though it is molded and shaped by custom and culture, has many of its roots in basic sensual appetites.

CHAPTER 4

DISEASES OF THE EAR

A variety of diseases or disorders can affect the human ear, often to the detriment of hearing or balance. Impaired hearing is, with rare exception, the result of disease or abnormality of the outer, middle, or inner ear. Serious impairment of hearing at birth almost always results from a dysfunction of the cochlear (or auditory) nerve and may not lend itself to improvement by medical or surgical treatment. In early and late childhood the most frequent cause for impaired hearing is poor functioning of the eustachian tubes with the accumulation of a clear, pale yellowish fluid in the middle-ear cavity, a disorder called serous, or secretory, otitis media. In early and middle adult life the usual cause for progressive impairment of hearing is otosclerosis. The usual cause of hearing loss after age 60 is presbycusis, a disorder that results from the aging process.

In most cases when loss of hearing is due to a problem with sound conduction, surgical restoration can correct the defect and restore hearing. When loss of hearing is the result of nerve damage, a device known as a cochlear implant may restore hearing to some degree. In severe cases, however, hearing loss may be permanent, with neither surgery nor an implanted device improving the condition.

More important than a cure for auditory nerve damage is prevention. Cases of deafness in the newborn due to rubella (German measles) in the mother can be averted with the rubella vaccine. Nerve damage caused by exposure to excessive and prolonged noise is preventable by early detection. One approach is to give routine hearing tests to individuals who work in environments where excessive noise is unavoidable.

The incidence of impaired hearing in the general population depends on the degree of hearing loss defined as impaired. According to U.S. statistics, by age 6, 0.2 percent of all children have impaired hearing in one or both ears that is sufficient to warrant consultation of an ear specialist. By age 18 the number of children with hearing loss sufficient to require diagnostic examination reaches 2.5 to 3 percent. By age 65 the number of adults with a recognizable hearing impairment reaches 5 percent. After age 65 the incidence of impaired hearing rises rapidly. About 30 to 35 percent of individuals between the ages of 65 and 75 and 40 percent of those older than 75 are affected by hearing loss.

Comparable figures from the United Kingdom show that 1 in 6 persons is estimated to have some hearing difficulty, but only one-fourth of these have any real handicap, with one-third of this latter group needing hearing aids and 1 in 20 being deaf to all speech. Of British children, 1 in 1,000 is severely deaf, and as many as 7 per 1,000 are estimated to have a level of impairment that requires some form of help.

DISEASES OF THE OUTER EAR

Diseases of the outer ear are those that afflict skin, cartilage, and the glands and hair follicles in the outer-ear canal. The sound-transmitting function of the outer ear is impaired when the ear canal becomes filled with tumour, infected material, or earwax (cerumen), so that sound cannot reach the tympanic membrane, or eardrum. The most common diseases of the outer ear are briefly described in the following paragraphs.

Infections and Injuries of the Outer Ear

The exposed position of the outer ear makes it the part of the body most frequently affected by freezing, or frostbite. Humidity, duration of exposure, and, most of all, wind, in addition to degrees of temperature below freezing, predispose to the occurrence of frostbite. The frozen area begins along the upper and outer edge of the ear, which becomes yellow-white and waxy in appearance, cold and hard to the touch, and numb with loss of skin sensation.

In treatment of frostbite the victim is placed as soon as possible in a warm room, but the frozen ear is kept cool by applying ice wrapped in a towel until the returning blood circulation gradually thaws the frozen part from within. Massage of the frozen ear is avoided, for it is likely to injure the skin. Heat applied to the frozen area before circulation is established can result in clotting of the blood in the blood vessels. This in turn can result in death of that part of the ear, which turns black and eventually falls off, a process called dry gangrene.

Injury to the outer ear can cause bleeding between the cartilage and the skin, producing a smooth, rounded, non-tender purplish swelling called hematoma. The accumulation of clotted blood is removed by a surgeon because, if it is left, it will become transformed into scar tissue and cause a permanent, irregular thickening of the outer ear commonly called cauliflower ear and seen in boxers and wrestlers whose ears receive much abuse.

Infection of the cartilage of the outer ear, called perichondritis, is unusual but may occur from injury or from swimming in polluted water. It is due to a particular microorganism, *Pseudomonas aeruginosa*. There is a greenish or brownish, musty or foul-smelling discharge from the outer-ear canal, while the affected outer ear becomes tender, dusky red, and two to three times its normal thickness. Prompt antibiotic treatment is necessary to prevent permanent deformity of the outer ear.

Infection of the outer-ear canal by molds or various microorganisms occurs especially in warm, humid climates and among swimmers. The ear canal itches and becomes tender, and a small amount of thin, often foul-smelling material drains from it. If the canal becomes clogged by the swelling and drainage, hearing will be impaired. Careful and thorough cleaning of the outer-ear canal by a physician, application of antiseptic or antibiotic eardrops, and avoidance of swimming are indicated to clear up the infection.

Infection of a hair follicle anywhere on the body is known as a boil, or furuncle. This can occur in a hair follicle in the outer-ear canal, especially when there is infection of the skin of the canal. It always occurs because of a particular type of germ known as staphylococcus. Because the skin of the ear canal is closely attached to the underlying cartilage, a boil in the ear canal is especially painful, with swelling, redness, and tenderness but generally without fever. Heat applied to the outer ear by a hot-water bottle or electric pad helps the infection to come to a head and begin to drain. Treatment with a systemic and local antibiotic is required to prevent other hair follicles from becoming infected.

Erysipelas is an infection in the skin caused by a particular type of streptococcus and characterized by a slowly advancing red, slightly tender thickening of the skin. It may begin at the ear and spread to the face and neck. Centuries ago erysipelas epidemics caused severe and often fatal infections. In 1089 CE one of the most severe erysipelas epidemics occurred. The disease was referred to as St. Anthony's fire because those who prayed to St. Anthony were said to recover; others, who did not, died.

Today erysipelas is usually a mild and comparatively rare infection that clears up rapidly when treated with an antibiotic.

Leprosy, seen rarely outside the tropics today, was another scourge of ancient times that sometimes affected the outer ear. It is caused by the leprosy bacillus, *Mycobacterium leprae*, which causes a painless, slowly progressing thickening and distortion of the affected tissues. The diagnosis is made by examining a bit of the infected tissue under a microscope and finding the leprosy bacilli, which in appearance are not unlike the bacilli that cause tuberculosis. Fortunately, the antibiotics effective against tuberculosis are effective today in arresting the progression of the disease.

Osteoma of the bony ear canal is a bony knob that grows close to the tympanic membrane, especially in those who swim a great deal in cold water. It is not dangerous and does not need to be removed unless the bony overgrowth becomes large enough to block the ear canal.

A cyst is a sac filled with liquid or semisolid material. A cyst of the ear is most often caused by a gland that lubricates the skin behind the earlobe, less often at the entrance of the ear canal. If the duct of this gland becomes stopped, the lubricating fatty material accumulates as a soft, rounded nodule in the skin. Infection of the cyst causes a tender abscess to form and drain. The cyst will re-form unless removed completely by surgery.

Another type of cyst occurs above the ear canal, just in front of the outer ear or, rarely, in the neck behind and below the ear. This is a remnant of the primitive gill of the early embryo, a reminder that humans share an evolutionary past with fishes. It may appear as a tiny pitlike depression that discharges a little moisture from time to time, or a cystic swelling may develop when the opening of the pit is closed, requiring surgical removal.

In dark-skinned people, overgrowth of scar tissue from any skin incision or injury can cause a thickened elevation on the scar called a keloid. Having the earlobes pierced for earrings sometimes results in a large, painless nodular keloid enlargement of the earlobe, harmless but unsightly. Keloids are removed surgically.

DEFORMITIES AND OTHER CONDITIONS OF THE OUTER EAR

Congenital deformity or absence of the outer ear, usually on one side, sometimes on both, is often accompanied by absence of the outer-ear canal. This failure of the primitive gill structures to become properly transformed into the normal outer and middle ear is, in rare instances, hereditary.

Five-year-old Peter Dankelson suffers from a congenital disease that robbed him of his left ear. A doctor shows him a prosthetic ear that has been created for him. Tim Sloan/AFP/Getty Images

More often it occurs for no known reason. In some cases it can be traced to the damaging effects on the embryo of rubella in the mother during the first three months of her pregnancy. Since the inner ear and nerves of equilibrium and hearing come from the otic vesicle, separate from the gill structure, in most cases of deformed or absent outer ear the hearing nerve is normal. Surgical construction of a new ear canal and tympanic membrane can often improve the hearing, which has been impaired by the failure of sound conduction to reach the hearing nerve in the inner ear.

Lop ear, excessive protrusion of the ear from the side of the head, is a more frequent but less serious deformity of the outer ear. Surgery may be performed to bring the ears back to a more normal and less conspicuous position.

Eczema of the skin of the outer ear, like eczema elsewhere, is an itching, scaling redness, sometimes with weeping of the affected skin. It is often the result of an allergy to a food or substance such as hair spray that comes in contact with the skin. The best treatment is discovery and avoidance of the allergen. Cortisone ointment applied topically may temporarily relieve symptoms.

The waxy substance produced by glands in the skin of the outer-ear canal normally is carried outward by slow migration to the outer layers of skin. When wax is produced too rapidly, it can accumulate, completely filling the outer-ear canal and blocking the passage of sound to the tympanic membrane, causing a painless impairment of hearing. Large plugs of earwax need to be removed by a physician. Smaller amounts may be softened by a a few drops of baby oil left in the ear overnight, then syringed out with warm water and a soft-rubber infant ear syringe.

Cancer of the outer ear occurs chiefly in instances where the outer ear has been exposed for many years to direct sunlight. A small and at first painless ulcer, with a dry scab covering it, that slowly enlarges and deepens may be a skin cancer. It is diagnosed by removing a small bit of tissue from the edge and examining it under a microscope. The cancerous tissue must be completely eradicated, by either surgery or radiation, to effect a cure. Cancer that arises in the ear canal is more serious, for it may invade the bone before it is diagnosed. It is then more difficult to cure by removal. Cancers of the ear canal are rather rare, while cancers of the skin of the outer ear are more common, as well as more readily cured by removal.

DISEASES OF THE MIDDLE EAR

The air-filled middle-ear cavity and the air cells in the mastoid bone that extend backward from it are supplied with air by the eustachian tube that extends from the upper part of the pharynx to the middle-ear cavity. The brain cavity lies just above and behind the middle ear and mastoid air spaces, separated from them only by thin plates of bone. The nerve that supplies the muscles of expression in the face passes through the middle-ear cavity and mastoid bone. It, too, is separated from them by only a thin layer of bone. In some instances this bony covering is incomplete, so that the facial nerve lies directly against the mucous membrane that lines the middle ear and mastoid air cells. This mucous membrane, an extension of a similar mucus-producing membrane that lines the nose and upper part of the throat, extends all the way through the eustachian tube into the middle ear and mastoid. It is subject to the same allergic reactions and infections that afflict the nasal passages. Thus, an acute head cold or other infection of the nose and throat, such as measles or scarlet fever, may extend through the eustachian tube into the middle ear and mastoid air cells.

The proximity of the brain cavity to the mastoid air cells is such that an infection, if severe and untreated, may lead to meningitis (inflammation of the covering of the brain) or brain abscess. The large vein that drains blood from the brain passes through the mastoid bone on its way to the jugular vein in the neck. Infection from the middle ear can extend to this vein, resulting in "blood poisoning" (infection of the bloodstream, also called septicemia). Paralysis of the facial nerve and infection extending from the middle ear to the labyrinth of the inner ear are other possible complications of middle-ear infection. All these possibilities spring from the particular location of the small but important middle-ear cavity.

ACUTE MIDDLE-EAR INFECTION

Fortunately, acute middle-ear infections, called acute otitis media, are nearly always due to microorganisms that respond quickly to antibiotics. As a result, acute infection of the mastoid air cells resulting in a dangerous mastoid abscess with the possibility of meningitis, brain abscess, septicemia, infection of the labyrinth, or facial nerve paralysis, complicating an acute infection of the middle-ear cavity, has become rare. Abscess of the mastoid and the other complications of acute middle-ear infection are seen chiefly in remote regions and countries where the population lacks proper nutrition and adequate medical care.

While serious and life-threatening acute infections of the middle ear and mastoid air cells have become rare, chronic infections, mentioned below, continue to occur, and another type of middle-ear disease, secretory otitis media, is frequent.

Secretory Otitis Media

In secretory otitis media the middle-ear cavity becomes filled with a clear, pale yellowish, noninfected fluid. The disorder is the result of inadequate ventilation of the middle ear through the eustachian tube. The air in the middle ear, when it is no longer replenished through this tube, is gradually absorbed by the mucous membrane, and fluid takes its place. Eventually, the middle-ear cavity is completely filled with fluid instead of air. The fluid impedes the vibratory movements of the tympanic membrane and the ossicular chain, causing a painless impairment of hearing.

The usual causes for secretory otitis media are an acute head cold with swelling of the membranes of the eustachian tube, an allergic reaction of the membranes in the eustachian tube, and an enlarged adenoid (nodule of lymphoid tissue) blocking the entrance to the eustachian tube. The condition is cured by finding and removing the cause and then removing the fluid from the middle-ear cavity, if it does not disappear by itself within a week or two. Removal of the fluid requires puncturing the tympanic membrane and forcing air through the eustachian tube to blow out the fluid. In the absence of fever and infection of the middle ear, antibiotics, which may impede the normal immune protection of the middle ear, are not necessary. In cases in which an allergic reaction is not the underlying cause of the condition, it may be necessary to insert a tiny plastic tube through the membrane to aid in reestablishing normal ventilation of the middle-ear cavity. After a time, when the middle ear and hearing have returned to normal, this plastic tube is removed. The small hole left in the tympanic membrane quickly heals.

Aero-Otitis Media

Aero-otitis media is a painful type of hearing loss that can result from an inability to equalize the air pressure in the middle-ear cavity when a sudden change in altitude occurs, as may happen in a rapid descent in a poorly pressurized aircraft. Allergies or a preexisting head cold may inhibit an individual's ability to equalize, which is accomplished by yawning or swallowing to open the eustachian tube. The tympanic membrane becomes sharply retracted when the air pressure becomes less within than without, while the opening of the tube into the upper part of the throat becomes pressed tightly together by the increased air pressure in the throat, so that the tube cannot be opened by swallowing. A severe sense of pressure in the ear is accompanied by pain and a decrease in hearing. Sometimes the tympanic membrane ruptures because of the difference in pressure on its two sides. More often, the pain continues until the middle ear fills with fluid or the membrane is surgically punctured. Usually aero-otitis media produced during a flight is of a temporary nature and disappears of its own accord.

CHRONIC MIDDLE-EAR INFECTION

Chronic infection of the middle ear occurs when there is a permanent perforation of the tympanic membrane that allows dust, water, and germs from the outer air to gain access to the middle-ear cavity. This results in a chronic drainage from the middle ear through the outer-ear canal. There are two distinct types of chronic middle-ear infection, one relatively harmless, the other caused by a dangerous bone-invading process that leads, when neglected, to serious complications.

The harmless type of chronic middle-ear disease is recognized by a stringy, odourless, mucoid discharge that comes from the surface of the mucous membrane that lines the middle ear. Medical treatment with applications of boric acid powder will dry up the chronic drainage. The perforation in the membrane may then be closed, restoring the normal structure and function of the ear with recovery of hearing.

The dangerous type of chronic middle-ear drainage is recognized by its foul-smelling discharge, often scanty in amount, coming from a bone-invading process beneath the mucous membrane. Such cases are usually caused by a condition known as cholesteatoma of the middle ear. This is an ingrowth of skin from the outer-ear canal that forms a cyst within the middle ear. An infected cholesteatoma cyst enlarges slowly but progressively, gradually eroding the bone until the cyst reaches the brain cavity, the nerve that supplies the muscles of the face, or a semicircular canal of the inner ear. The infected material within the cyst then produces a serious complication: meningitis or brain abscess, paralysis of the facial nerve, or infection of the labyrinth of the inner ear with vertigo, all of which may lead to total deafness.

Fortunately, cholesteatoma of the middle ear is now rarely so neglected as to permit development of a serious complication. By careful examination of the tympanic membrane perforation and by X-ray studies, the bone-eroding cyst can be diagnosed. It can then be removed surgically before it has caused serious harm. This operation is known as a radical mastoid or a modified radical mastoid operation. If during the same procedure the perforation in the tympanic membrane is closed and the ossicular chain repaired, the operation is known as a tympanoplasty, or plastic reconstruction of the middle-ear cavity.

OSSICULAR INTERRUPTION

The ossicular chain of three tiny bones needed to carry sound vibrations from the tympanic membrane to the fluid that fills the inner ear may be disrupted by infection or by a jarring blow on the head. Most often the separation occurs at its weakest point, where the incus joins the stapes. If the separation is partial, there is a mild impairment of hearing. If it is complete, there is a severe hearing loss. In such a case, a hearing test demonstrates that the nerve of hearing in the inner ear is functioning normally but that sound fails to be conducted from the tympanic membrane to the inner ear. The defective ossicular chain can be surgically corrected through tympanoplasty, which allows sound to be conducted to the inner ear once again.

Otosclerosis

The commonest cause for progressive hearing loss in early and middle adult life is a disease of the hard shell of bone that surrounds the labyrinth of the inner ear. This disease of bone is known as otosclerosis, a name that is misleading, for in its early and actively expanding stage the nodule of diseased bone is softer than the ivory-hard bone that it replaces. The more appropriate name otospongiosis is sometimes used, but such is the tenacity of tradition that the older name, applied before the process was well understood, has persisted and is the term generally used.

The cause for the occurrence of the nodule of softened otosclerotic bone is unknown. There is a certain familial tendency, half the cases occurring in families in which one or several relatives have the same condition. It is one-tenth as common among blacks as among whites and twice as common in women as in men. The nodule of softened otosclerotic bone first appears in late childhood or in early adult life. Fortunately, in most cases it remains quite small and harmless, producing no symptoms, and is discoverable only if the ear bones are removed after death and examined under a microscope. Such evidence indicates that approximately 1 in 10 white adult men and 1 in 5 white adult women will be found to have such a nodule of otosclerotic bone by middle adult life.

In about 12 percent of otosclerosis cases the nodule of softened bone becomes large enough to reach the oval window containing the footplate of the stapes (stirrup). Increasing pressure caused by the expanding nodule begins to impede its vibratory movements in response to sound striking the tympanic membrane. Gradually and insidiously, affected persons begin to lose their sharpness of hearing. First they begin to lose the ability to hear faint sounds of low pitch, next they begin to have difficulty hearing the whispered voice, then they have difficulty in hearing conversation from a distance, and finally they can hear and understand the spoken voice only when it is quite loud or close to the ear. One of the characteristics of impaired hearing due to stirrup fixation by otosclerosis is retained ability to hear a telephone conversation by pressing the receiver against the head so that the sound is carried to the inner ear by bone conduction. Another characteristic of this type of impaired hearing is that hearing seems to improve while one is riding in an automobile, in a plane, or on a train. This is because the low-pitched roar of motors causes persons with normal hearing to unconsciously raise their voices, while the individual with stirrup fixation fails to hear the low-pitched roar and thus hears better and enjoys the raised voices.

The diagnosis of stirrup fixation by otosclerosis is made on the basis of a history of a gradually increasing impairment of hearing with absence of any chronic infection of the middle ear or of perforation of the tympanic membrane and with hearing tests showing that the auditory nerve in the inner ear is functioning but that sound fails to be conducted properly to it. Hearing tests carried out with either a tuning fork or an audiometer demonstrate that the hearing by bone conduction is better than by air conduction.

The final and conclusive diagnosis of otosclerosis is a finding made through surgical exploration—namely, that the stapes is fixed and unable to be moved because of a nodule of bone that has grown against it. An X ray of the ear using computed tomography may be made to demonstrate that the footplate of the stapes has been invaded by otosclerosis.

Fixation of the stapes can be corrected surgically. In 1956 it was found that the fixed stapes could be removed and replaced by a plastic or wire substitute in cases in which it could not be mobilized. Today this operation, known as stapedectomy, is the one most often used to correct fixation of the stapes by otosclerosis.

The otosclerotic bone disease in some cases expands as far as the cochlea of the inner ear, causing a gradual deterioration of the auditory nerve. This progressive nerve deafness may precede, accompany, or follow fixation of the stapes. In some cases it may occur without fixation of the stapes.

While the exact cause of otosclerosis is not known, it may be associated in some cases with lack of fluoride in drinking water. There is evidence that increasing the intake of fluoride may promote hardening of the softened nodule of otosclerotic bone, thus arresting or retarding its expansion. In this way the gradual impairment of auditory nerve function that often occurs with fixation of the stapes may be retarded. Fluoridation of water supplies, which is carried out in many countries, has reduced the incidence of otosclerosis.

DISEASES OF THE INNER EAR

Diseases of the labyrinth of the inner ear may affect both the vestibular nerve and the auditory nerve, or they may affect only the auditory nerve, with loss of hearing, or the vestibular nerve, bringing on vertigo. Examples of inner ear diseases include congenital nerve deafness and viral nerve deafness. About 1 in every 1,000 infants demonstrates profound congenital hearing loss.

CONGENITAL NERVE DEAFNESS

Congenital nerve deafness, a defect of the auditory nerve in the cochlea, may be present at birth or acquired during or soon after birth. Usually both inner ears are affected to a similar degree, and as a rule there is a severe impairment of hearing, although in some cases of congenital nerve loss the impairment is moderate.

Congenital nerve deafness acquired at or soon after birth may result from insufficient oxygen (anoxia) during a difficult and prolonged delivery or from the condition known as kernicterus, in which the baby becomes jaundiced because of incompatibility between its blood and that of the mother. However, in the past, many cases of congenital nerve deafness were caused by the rubella virus in the mother during the first three months of her pregnancy, causing arrest of development of the vesicle of the embryo. This can happen during a rubella epidemic, even when the mother has no symptoms of the infection. In most cases the vestibular nerve is not affected or is affected to a lesser degree, and in most (but not all) cases the outer- and middle-ear structures are not affected. A vaccine against the rubella virus made available in 1969 has reduced the number of cases of congenital nerve deafness in developed countries.

In a few cases congenital nerve deafness is an inherited failure of the cochlea to develop properly. When the hearing loss is severe, speech cannot be acquired without special training. Children so afflicted must attend special classes or schools for the severely deaf, where they can be taught lipreading, speech, and sign language. Electrical hearing aids can be helpful, especially during classes, to use the remnants of hearing usually present in such cases. Another alternative, although controversial within the deaf community, is a cochlear implant, which is sometimes useful in cases of profound hearing loss or total absence of hearing when the nerve itself is present. In this operation an electrode is surgically implanted to directly stimulate the auditory nerve between the brain and the ear.

Most hearing loss, especially among older adults, is not considered genetic in origin but is typically the result of accumulated damage from trauma or infection. On the other hand, a majority of the cases of isolated hearing loss—hearing loss unaccompanied by other symptoms (such as blindness)—seen in young infants are genetic. Recent studies show that hearing loss in these infants is the result of mutations in one or more of an extraordinary number of different genes. Identification of the relevant genes and mutations has given powerful insight into the broad range of gene products that must function together to achieve normal hearing. They include intracellular motor proteins, ion channels and pumps, transcription factors that regulate the expression of other genes, and extracellular matrix proteins that help to form the tectorial membrane of the inner ear. More will likely be identified in the years to come. Perhaps the mutated genes seen most often in these patients, however, are those that code for the connexins. Connexins are gap junction proteins—proteins spanning the cell membrane that control the passage of small molecules directly from the interior of one cell to that of another. These gap junction proteins contribute to the communication between supporting, nonsensory cells of the inner ear. Mutations in the gene *CX26*, which codes for the protein connexin 26, account for almost half of all cases of isolated congenital deafness in Caucasian populations.

Knowledge of the identities and functions of these genes and their products leads to improved early diagnosis, which in turn offers improved options for intervention, including cochlear implants. Early diagnosis followed by prompt intervention is important because the auditory regions of the brains of infants born with profound hearing loss will not develop properly unless hearing is restored quickly. Partly in recognition of this urgency, congenital hearing loss has joined the list of other, mostly metabolic, impairments for which newborn screening procedures are mandated in some U.S. states and other parts of the world.

VIRAL NERVE DEAFNESS

Viral infections can cause severe degrees of sensorineural hearing loss in one ear, and sometimes in both, at any age. The mumps virus is one of the commonest causes of severe sensorineural hearing loss in one ear. The measles and influenza viruses are less-common causes. There is no effective medical or surgical treatment to restore hearing impaired by a virus.

EFFECTS OF INJURY AND TRAUMA

The middle and inner ear are subject to injury and trauma from any of a number of causes. The most common injury is the loss of hearing from exposure to excessive noise. Such exposures can occur in a range of settings but generally are experienced in industrial facilities. Noise produced by highway, railway, and airplane traffic can also be problematic for persons who may be routinely exposed to the sounds. Injury and trauma to the ear may also be caused by certain drugs or by skull fracture and concussion.

Ototoxic Drugs

Ototoxic (harmful to the ear) drugs can cause temporary and sometimes permanent impairment of auditory nerve function. Salicylates such as aspirin in large enough doses may cause ringing in the ears and then a temporary decrease in hearing that ceases when the person stops taking the drug. Quinine can have a similar effect but with a permanent impairment of auditory nerve function in some cases. Certain antibiotics, such as streptomycin, dihydrostreptomycin, neomycin, and kanamycin, may cause permanent damage to auditory nerve function. Susceptibility to auditory nerve damage from ototoxic drugs varies greatly among individuals. In most cases, except when streptomycin is the drug taken, the more durable and less easily damaged vestibular nerve is not affected. Streptomycin affects the vestibular nerve more than it affects the auditory nerve.

Skull Fracture and Concussion

Skull fracture and concussion from a severe blow on the head can impair the functioning of the auditory and vestibular nerves in varying degrees. The greatest hearing loss arises when a fracture of the skull passes through the labyrinth of the inner ear, totally destroying its function.

Exposure to Noise

The effects of noise exposure on hearing depend on the intensity and duration of the noise. The effects may be temporary or permanent. A single exposure to an extremely intense sound, such as an explosion, may produce a severe and permanent loss of hearing. Repeated exposures to sounds in excess of 80 to 90 decibels may cause gradual deterioration of hearing by destroying the hair cells of the inner ear, with possible subsequent degeneration of nerve fibres. The levels of noise produced by rock music bands frequently exceed 110 decibels. The noise generated by farm tractors, power mowers, and snowmobiles may reach 100 decibels. In the United States, legislation requires that workers exposed to sound levels greater than 90 decibels for an eight-hour day be provided some form of protection, such as earplugs or earmuffs.

Individuals differ in their susceptibility to hearing loss from noise exposure. Because hearing loss typically begins at the higher frequencies of 4,000 to 6,000 hertz, the effects of noise exposure may go unnoticed until the hearing loss spreads to the lower frequencies of 1,000 to 2,000

A man covers his ears in Colombo, Sri Lanka, as firecrackers are lit during the April 8, 2010, presidential election. Loud noises can profoundly damage ears. Ishara S. Kodikara/AFP/Getty Images

hertz. Inhalation of carbogen, a mixture of 5 percent carbon dioxide and 95 percent oxygen, for 20 minutes will accelerate recovery of hearing if administered within a few hours after excessive noise exposure.

INFLAMMATION AND TUMOURS

Inflammation of the ear is fairly common and may be primary, arising from a condition of the ear itself, or secondary, being caused by an underlying infection or other disorder. Examples of conditions involving inflammation of the ear include labyrinthitis, Ménière disease, and tinnitus. An example of a tumour of the ear is acoustic neuroma, which can affect hearing and produce a range of neurological symptoms.

ACOUSTIC NEUROMA

An acoustic neuroma is a benign tumour that grows on the auditory nerve near the point where it enters the labyrinth of the inner ear. The tumour causes gradual and progressive loss of auditory and vestibular nerve function on one side. Eventually the tumour grows out into the brain cavity, causing headaches and paralysis. If it is not removed, blindness and death may result. Fortunately, acoustic neuroma usually can be diagnosed early by magnetic resonance imaging (MRI) and removed before it has serious consequences.

LABYRINTHITIS

Labyrinthitis, an inflammation of the labyrinth of the inner ear, happens when infection occurs as a result of meningitis, syphilis, acute otitis media and mastoiditis, or chronic otitis media and cholesteatoma. Loss of both equilibrium and hearing occurs in the affected ear. Prompt antibiotic treatment sometimes arrests the damage and allows for the possibility of partial recovery of the function of the inner ear.

Ménière Disease

Ménière disease, also called endolymphatic hydrops, is a fairly common disorder of the labyrinth of the inner ear that affects both the vestibular nerve, with resultant attacks of vertigo, and the auditory nerve, with impairment of hearing. It was first described in 1861 by a French physician, Prosper Ménière. It is now known that the symptoms are caused by an excess of endolymphatic fluid in the inner ear.

The diagnosis is made from the recurring attacks of vertigo, often with nausea and vomiting, impairment of hearing with a distortion of sound in the affected ear that fluctuates in degree, and a sense of fullness or pressure in the ear. The cause of the excess of endolymphatic fluid is not always known, although in many cases it results from defective functioning of the endolymphatic duct and sac, the structures that normally resorb endolymphatic fluid from the inner ear.

Allergic reactions to certain foods may also cause the disease. The treatment of Ménière disease is directed toward finding the cause of the excess of endolymphatic fluid in order to control it. If medical treatment does not relieve the repeated attacks of vertigo, surgery may be necessary.

Presbycusis

Presbycusis is the gradual decline of hearing function that results from aging. It is similar to other aging processes because it occurs at different ages and at different rates among the population. As a person ages, there is a gradual loss of cochlear hair cells, beginning at the basal end of the organ of Corti, with the result that hearing is gradually reduced and eventually lost, first for the highest audible frequencies (around 20,000 hertz) and then progressively for sounds of lower frequency. Usually the slow diminishing of hearing does not begin until after age 60. The affected individual notices increasing difficulty in hearing sounds of high pitch and in understanding conversation.

Correction of a nutritional deficiency of zinc, coenzyme Q_{10}, or possibly vitamin A may stabilize the progressive hearing loss. The physician must make certain that the individual does not have a correctable impairment, such as accumulated earwax, secretory otitis media, or stirrup fixation by otosclerosis, as part of the difficulty. An electrical hearing aid is of limited help to some, while others find that a hearing aid makes voices louder but less clear and therefore is of little help.

TINNITUS

Tinnitus is a ringing or buzzing in the ears. An estimated one-third of adults experience tinnitus at some point in their lives, and some 10 to 15 percent of individuals are afflicted by chronic tinnitus. There are two types of tinnitus: subjective, which is the most common form, and objective, which is relatively rare. In subjective tinnitus, only the person with the condition can hear the noise. In objective tinnitus, a physician can detect the ringing, buzzing, or clicking sound.

The perceived ringing sound in the ears that characterizes tinnitus may be caused by any of a number of ear conditions, including the clogging of the external auditory canal with earwax (cerumen) or inflammation of

Audiologist Rebecca Price, left, uses special equipment to test patient Teri Kim for tinnitus at Duke Hospital in Durham, North Carolina. Raleigh News & Observer/McClatchy-Tribune/Getty Images

the eardrum membrane, the middle ear, or the inner ear. Tinnitus may also result from exposure to noise, from taking high doses of certain drugs (such as aspirin or the malaria drug chloroquine), or from excessive use of the telephone. It may accompany hearing loss, particularly in the high-frequency range. Tinnitus can also be caused by hypertension (abnormally high blood pressure), atherosclerosis (the accumulation of fat and cholesterol in the inner layer of arteries), and tumours of the cranial nerve (acoustic neuroma) or tumours that place pressure on blood vessels in the head or neck. Ringing in the ears sometimes accompanies vertigo (dizziness). Despite these known factors, there is no cause identified for the majority of persons with tinnitus. Tinnitus may become more pronounced when the affected individual is fatigued, and it is often more obvious at night than during the day.

Treatment of tinnitus may involve simply removing excess earwax or terminating the use of medications that can cause the condition. Surgery may be needed to correct vascular disorders that give rise to tinnitus. Hearing aids, noise suppression devices, and similar approaches may be used to mask the obviousness of the ringing or buzzing sound. Music therapy, in which a patient listens to music that lacks notes equivalent in frequency to the ringing sound the patient hears, has been shown to alleviate the perceived loudness of chronic tinnitus in some individuals. In severe cases, drugs such as alprazolam and amitriptyline may be prescribed to reduce the symptoms of tinnitus.

CHAPTER 5

COMMUNICATION DISORDERS INVOLVING STRUCTURES OF THE EAR, NOSE, AND THROAT

Human communication relies largely on the faculty of speech, supplemented by the production of certain sounds, each of which is unique in meaning. Human speech is extraordinarily complex, consisting of sound waves of a diverse range of frequencies, intensities, and amplitudes that convey specific information. The production and reception of these sounds requires a properly functioning ear and auditory system, as well as intact and healthy vocal and sound-generating structures, including the larynx, tongue, and lips.

Vocal communication can be rendered difficult or impossible due to deformities in the physical structures used in speech and sound production or to disorders affecting areas of the brain that process speech and sound. Communication disorders can be divided into three main categories: speech, voice, and articulation disorders. The latter group includes some of the most common and well-known speech disorders, namely, lisping and stuttering.

PREVALENCE OF COMMUNICATION DISORDERS

In the United States, statistics from the early 21st century compiled by the National Institute on Deafness and Other Communication Disorders revealed that approximately

36 million Americans had experienced hearing loss of some degree and that some 5 percent of American children had detectable speech disorders by age 6 or 7. In addition, about 7.5 million Americans were found to be unable to use their voice normally. Many of these individuals struggled to perceive the loudness, pitch, or quality of sound they produced with the voice. Disorders of articulation among young children were the most frequent disorders of communication.

Studies in Germany, Austria, and other central European countries suggest that the incidence and prevalence of speech disorders follow patterns similar to those observed among other Western countries. There are, however, deviations from these trends. Studies of stuttering that have focused on specific populations, including Americans, Europeans, and Africans, have indicated that the prevalence of the disorder among these populations is highly variable. However, generalization of the data suggests that roughly 2.5 percent of children under age 5 are affected by stuttering. For some speech disorders, reliable data on global prevalence and distribution is lacking.

SPEECH DISORDERS

In accordance with physiological considerations, disorders of communication are first classified into disorders of voice and phonic respiration, disorders of articulated speech, and disorders of language. It has been known for a long time that the majority of communication disorders are not caused by local lesions of the teeth, tongue, vocal cords, or regulating brain centres. Since these predominant disorders of voice and speech develop from derangements of the underlying physiological functions of breathing, use of the voice, speaking habits, or emotional disorders, this group has been labelled as functional.

The remainder of the communication disorders with clearly recognizable structural abnormalities in the total speech mechanism has been labeled organic.

While this empirical grouping has certain implications for the selection of the appropriate treatment, it is not satisfactory because organic structure and living function can never be separated. Certain functional disorders of the voice caused by its habitual abuse may very well lead to secondary structural changes, such as the growths (polyps and nodules) of the vocal cords, which develop as a result of vocal abuse. On the other hand, all of the obviously organic and structural lesions, such as loss of the tongue from accident or surgery, almost inevitably will be followed by emotional and other psychological reactions. In this case, the functional components are of secondary nature but to a great extent will influence the total picture of disturbance, including the patient's ability to adjust to the limitation, to relearn a new mode of appropriate function, and to make the best of his or her condition.

Within these major groups, the various types of communication disorders have for a long time, and in most parts of the world, been described by the listener's perceptual impression. Most languages employ specific words for the various types of abnormal speech, such as stuttering, stammering, cluttering, mumbling, lisping, whispering, and many others. The problem with such subjective and symptomatic labels is the fact that they try to define the final, audible result, the recognizable phenomenon, and not by any means the underlying basis. This general human tendency to describe disorders of communication by what the listener hears is analogous to the attempts of early medicine to classify diseases by the patient's symptoms that the diagnosing physician could see or hear or feel or perhaps smell. Before the great discoveries of the 19th century had erected a logical basis for medical pathology, the various diseases were classified as numerous types of fevers, congestions, and dyscrasias. Thus, malaria was originally thought to be caused by the evil emanations (miasma) of the bad air (*mal aria*) near swamps until it was recognized to be caused by a blood parasite transmitted by the mosquito.

The various approaches of medical, psychiatric, psychological, educational, behavioral, and other schools of speech pathology have made great advances in the recent past and better systems of classification continue to be proposed. They aim at grouping the observable symptoms of speech disorders according to the underlying origins instead of the listener's subjective impressions. While this is relatively easy in the case of language loss from, for example, a brain stroke because the destroyed brain areas can be identified at autopsy, it is more difficult in the case of the large group of so-called functional speech disorders for two reasons: first, they are definitely not caused by gross, easily visible organic lesions, and, second, many functional disorders are outgrown through maturation or appropriate learning (laboratory study of the involved tissues in such cases would reveal no detectable lesions). It is hoped that refined methods of study in the areas of both "functional" psychology and "organic" neurophysiology will eventually reveal the structural bases for the prevalent disorders of voice and speech.

VOICE DISORDERS

In international terminology, disorders of the voice are described as dysphonia. Depending on the underlying cause, the various types of dysphonia are subdivided by the specifying adjective. Thus, a vocal disorder stemming from paralysis of the larynx is a paralytic dysphonia; injury (trauma) of the larynx may produce traumatic dysphonia;

Arman, who has cerebral palsy, pronounces words with help from a speech therapist in 2009 in Bhopal, India. Twenty-five years after a massive gas leak, many Bhopal children are disabled. Daniel Berehulak/Getty Images

endocrine dysphonia reflects the voice changes resulting from disease of the various endocrine glands such as the pituitary. The various dysphonias of clearly organic origin from systemic disease (e.g., muscular, nervous, or degenerative disease afflicting the entire body) or from local laryngeal changes differ in their visible symptomatology, as well as in the perceptual impression produced by the abnormal voice. Nevertheless, it has not yet been possible to define the acoustical alterations in the vocal spectrum that would allow a clear and objective differentiation among the subjective graduations of an abnormal voice as hoarse, harsh, husky, breathy, grating, gravelly, or gritty.

Because a large group of dysphonias have no visible laryngeal causes, they are grouped as nonorganic. Two main types of these so-called functional voice disorders may be distinguished: the habitual dysphonias that arise from faulty speaking habits and the psychogenic dysphonias that stem from emotional causes. Both of these types of dysphonia again occur in two basic subtypes, the hyperkinetic (overactive) and the hypokinetic (underactive) since emotional disorders interfere with voluntary vocal function by causing either excessive or depressed physiological activity. In the hyperkinetic disorders, the highly coordinated patterns of phonation regress to the primitive, forceful, and exaggerated sphincter action of the larynx as seen during gagging. The result is hyperkinetic dysphonia, the gratingly harsh vocal disorder due to excessive muscular action in a constricted larynx. In the second subtype, the movements for phonation regress even more deeply to the original function of respiration. The sluggish larynx remains more or less open, and the glottis is incompletely closed for phonation, leading to hypokinetic dysphonia with subdued, breathy huskiness.

ARTICULATION DISORDERS

Disorders of articulation are characterized by abnormalities in the structure and function of the organs of speech, such as the tongue and lips. In many instances, these disorders are mechanical in nature, such as when the tongue interferes with the movement of the teeth or lips to cause lisping. Examples of articulation disorders include cluttering, lisping, and stuttering (or stammering).

CLUTTERING

A peculiar impediment of speech, cluttering (or tachyphemia) is characterized by hasty, sloppy, erratic, stumbling, jerky, and poorly intelligible speech that may somewhat resemble stuttering but differs from it markedly in that the clutterer is usually unaware of it, remains unconcerned, and does not seem to fear speaking situations. Its association with other past or persistent signs of subnormal language development differentiates congenital cluttering from emotional stuttering. Experts are strikingly unanimous in stressing the hereditary nature of cluttering.

Lisping

Although lisping belongs among the articulatory disorders and usually has the same causes as articulatory disorders in general, it differs from other disorders of articulation in several respects. For one, lisping occurs in various varieties, such as with the tongue tip protruding between the front teeth, with a slurping noise in the cheek pouch, with the tongue too far back along the palatal midline, with excessive tongue pressure against the teeth. There are also several snorting and nasal subtypes, and hissing deep in the throat or even within the larynx, such as in cleft-palate speech, may cause lisping. Moreover, the causes of lisping include a diverse group of particular conditions: abnormal number or position of teeth; imitation of other lispers; deficiency of palatal closure; slight hearing loss in the high frequencies; as well as several psychologic causes, such as effeminate affectation, infantile mannerisms, or mental disturbance. Lisping is less easily outgrown than the other infantile dyslalias (articulation disorders) and may persist into adult life if not corrected.

Stuttering, or Stammering

Academically known as dysphemia, what is called stuttering in the United States is usually named stammering in the United Kingdom. While everyone seems to know what stuttering sounds like, experts do not agree about what really causes it. In the age groups after puberty, stuttering is the most frequent and conspicuous type of disturbed speech encountered. This is one reason why among the studies dealing with speech pathology in the world literature those devoted to stuttering are the largest single group.

Despite numerous and intensive studies of the problem, findings and conclusions are far from unanimous. A great number of theories have been proposed to explain the origin and nature of stuttering, which range from the premise that subtle physical disturbances in the nervous system (so-called neurogenic asynchronies) are

The Duke of York and his family in Scotland in 1935. The Duke, who later became Britain's King George VI, received extensive speech therapy for his severe stuttering problem. Popperfoto/Getty Images

responsible to the opinion that psychological maladjustment alone is to blame.

Research findings indicate (as is the case with many developmental speech disorders, particularly language disability, articulatory disorders, reading disability, and cluttering) that trouble with stuttering affects the male sex two to four times more frequently than the female. Hereditary predisposition has been noted in many studies of large groups of stutterers, with evidence for an inherited tendency found among as many as 40 percent of the stutterers studied. Some experts insist that stuttering is not a single disease entity but that it comprises several types of the disorder with different causes. According to such views, the familial occurrence of stuttering represents a combination of the stuttering symptom with a cluttering tendency that is inherited. Although imitation of another stutterer may form the basis for acquiring the habit, purely psychological explanations that stress parental attitudes in training their children fail to reveal why many stutterers have siblings (brothers or sisters) with perfectly normal speech.

The treatment of stuttering is difficult and often demands much skill and responsibility on the part of the therapist. There is no medical cure for stuttering. For a time it was hoped that new psychopharmacological drugs (e.g., tranquillizers) might facilitate and accelerate recovery from stuttering. Although these efforts have not produced a pharmacological treatment thus far, several therapeutic approaches have been developed that can improve an affected individual's speech. The typical approach in this disorder is a strict program of psychotherapy (talking freely with a psychiatrist or psychologist so as to reduce emotional problems) supported by various applications of learning theory or behavioral theory (in retraining the stutterer) and other techniques depending on the therapist's position. It is widely agreed that the patient must acquire a better adjustment to the problems of his or her life and that he or she needs to develop a technique for controlling symptoms and fears. Prognosis (predicted outcome of treatment) thus is held to depend greatly on the patient's motivation and perseverance. It is interesting to note that experienced investigators no longer aspire to a "cure" of stuttering through an etiologic (causal) approach. Instead of focusing on underlying causes, they aim at making the patient "symptom-free" via symptomatic therapy.

Prevention of stuttering may be aided through parent counselling. The normal, immature speech of many children is characterized by various nonfluencies. These include hesitations, syllable repetition, groping for the right word, and vocalizations between words such as "ah-ah." Some misguided parents castigate these normal signs of developing speech with various admonitions and, even worse, try to forbid the nonfluencies by mislabelling them as stuttering. In some children, this parental interference associates normal nonfluency with feelings of insecurity and fear, tending to make the child become a real stutterer. Much research has been devoted to this probable etiology for one type of stuttering. Its elimination through parental guidance indeed has been reported to help in reducing the number of stutterers.

SPEECH OF THE HARD OF HEARING

Hearing loss that dates from childhood hinders the normal development of language because the most important sensory portal for speech learning remains deficient. Such children learn to say the sounds of speech as they hear them—in a muffled, distorted, or even inaudible fashion. The articulatory disorder (audiogenic dyslalia) usually reflects the measured (audiometric) pattern of hearing loss. If sound waves at high frequencies cannot be heard, speech sounds with formants in that high-frequency region will be affected. The hissing sibilants contain the highest formants and are therefore most typically disturbed by high-frequency hearing loss. The lower frequencies that can still be heard limit the audible formants to this residual range, which transposes the normal formant patterns into the abnormally lowered frequency band. As a result, a sharp hissing S is spoken as a muted Sh, and the light vowels are transformed into their darker counterparts (for example, the word "set" may be pronounced as "shot" or "shöd" as if it were German).

The voice reflects analogous changes. In the case of conductive hearing loss (in which neural structures for hearing are intact), the patient hears himself or herself well through the bones of the skull but cannot hear others. Because bone conduction remains good, the individual will perceive his or her own voice as being loud and hence tends to keep it subdued. The opposite occurs with neural (or perceptive) hearing loss in which there is nerve dysfunction. In this case, the patient hears his or her own voice as poorly as that of others and tends to talk in an overloud and screeching voice. Correction of audiogenic dyslalia may be possible through early fitting of a suitable hearing aid, intensive auditory training, and speech exercises aided by audiovisual playback devices (auditory trainers, tape recorders, visible speech devices, etc.).

Profound or total deafness going back to early childhood without special training inevitably leads to the absence of oral language development. Deaf children have traditionally been educated in special schools for the deaf, where the oral method (showing how to shape the oral structures for each speech sound) of teaching speech has competed with the older manual method of allowing the deaf to communicate through their own gestural or finger spelling. Advances in training include the liberal use of amplification devices (e.g., group hearing aids) in all school situations as well as the earliest possible fitting of hearing aids following definite diagnosis. This can be accomplished even when the patient cannot communicate that he or she hears (e.g., in very young babies) through methods such as recording brain-wave patterns in response to measured sound stimulation (EEG response audiometry).

SPEECH IMPEDIMENTS FROM DEFECTIVE ARTICULATORS

Dysglossic (from defective oral structures) disorders in articulation have interested humankind for the longest time. The biblical and poetical interchange of the words for "tongue" and "speech" in many languages has kept alive the assumption that speech originates within the fleshy tongue. For the same reason, the popular term *tongue-tied* still persists to refer to an abnormally immobile tongue and some assumed resulting limitation of linguistic ability. Even the academic designation of the science of languages as "linguistic" is traditionally based on the Latin word *lingua* for tongue.

TONGUE-TIE

In practice, the condition of a true tongue-tie (ankyloglossia) occurs only rarely and is quite easily corrected through a simple operation. Even when the shortened band beneath the tongue tip is permitted to persist, very little speech disturbance, if any, is audible in such persons. The only limitation of articulation to be expected is the decreased ability to protrude the tongue tip between the teeth for the English Th and the trilling lingual R in southern German, Latin, and Slavic languages. In any event, a true tongue-tie never causes stuttering, lisping, or any other of the major speech disorders.

LOSS OF TONGUE

Major defects of the tongue from paralysis, injury, or surgery reduce the articulation of the lingual sounds to the same extent that the tongue's mobility is visibly limited. Spontaneous compensation is usually quite prompt, depending on the patient's general linguistic talent. One exception is complete bilateral (both sides) paralysis of the tongue, which causes a very severe disorder of chewing and swallowing as well as severe limitation of speech intelligibility. The total loss of the tongue (true aglossia) from injury or surgery is often amazingly well compensated. Patients can learn to use residual portions of a tongue stump as well as other oral structures to substitute for the missing tongue. Indeed, some persons without a tongue have relearned to speak so well that the listener would not suspect its absence.

NASAL SPEECH

Several types of nasal speech are not easily diagnosed. Even specialized physicians are often not fully aware of the differences.

Increased nasal resonance leads to open nasality (hypernasal speech), affecting all oral speech sounds that should not be nasal. Organic causes impair the accuracy of palatal occlusion during emission of the nonnasal sounds. Among these are paralysis, congenital malformation, injury, or defects of the palate. The functional causes of palatal sluggishness include imitation, faulty speech habits, dialectal influences, hearing loss, mental retardation, or psychiatric disorders.

Decreased nasal resonance produces closed nasality (hyponasal speech), which muffles the three nasal resonants (M, N, and Ng). The best known organic causes are an acute cold, hay fever, large adenoids, and all other nasal diseases that obstruct the airway. Functional causes are less frequent, in the form of a rare, faulty speech habit. Occasionally the problem comes from intellectual disability or from severe language disability.

Mixed nasality poses a serious problem. It stems from the combination of one cause of open nasality with another of closed nasality (one may be of organic type and the other functional, or both may be organic). A typical combination is the open nasality from paralysis (paresis) of the palate (or its congenital deficiency) combined with closed nasality from obstruction of the nasopharynx by adenoids. The resulting mixed nasality causes the nasal resonants to sound muffled and subdued, while careful testing reveals slight open nasality on all oral sounds.

Treatment of nasal speech is unlikely to be successful without prudent balancing of all factors involved. This responsibility rests primarily with the diagnosing otolaryngologist or phoniatrist. The complaint of "talking through the nose" should never warrant a tonsil and adenoid operation without complete evaluation. If this were done in the example cited just above, removal of the obstructing adenoids would alleviate only the closed nasality, while making the open component more severe with marked deterioration of the patient's speech. This dilemma is often present when adenoids cause chronic middle-ear disease with hearing loss, while the palate is incompetent, as from a slight congenital malformation or paresis. In such case, the patient's general health and his or her hearing must be weighed against the possibility of making his or her speech worse.

Cleft Palate Speech

This type of organic dysglossia has also been named rhino-glossia (Greek *rhin, rhis*: "nose") because it is an organic cause of excessively nasal speech. Clefts of the lip, upper jaw, and hard and soft palate occur in various types and combinations. Cleft palate is a congenital (present at birth) malformation that develops for various reasons during the early weeks of embryonic life. The causes may be grouped as follows: inheritance in some cases; embryonal damage from various environmental causes in others; while still other cases of cleft palate are part of a syndrome of general or multiple malformation, which may again be hereditary, the result of chromosomal aberrations, or of environmental origin. Genetic influences are inferred from evidence that North American Indians (Montana) show a high incidence of cleft palate, but blacks (as on the island of Jamaica) show an unusually low incidence.

The speech disorder in cleft palate cases is complex. As a direct, mechanical result of the absent velopharyngeal (soft palate-pharynx) closure, voiced sounds assume an abnormal nasal quality from the unusual resonance of the nasal chambers. The influence of nasality on the perceptual and acoustic characteristics of the speech sounds has been discussed earlier. A second component is a mechanical limitation in articulating plosive sounds (e.g., P) because the necessary intra-oral pressure cannot be achieved. For the same reason, the sibilant sounds (e.g., S) are greatly distorted because the articulating air escapes through the nose before it can produce the characteristic hissing noise at one of the places of constriction. The child with an unrepaired cleft palate seems unconsciously to attempt to overcome these mechanical limitations in several ways. He or she tries to constrict the nostrils through facial grimaces and attempts to increase the expiratory air pressure. The child also succumbs to the "law of centripetal regression of articulation"—he or she shifts the articulation of the oral sounds below the point of deficient palatal occlusion, down into the pharynx or even the larynx. It is easy to demonstrate by X-ray fluoroscopy how the larynx becomes constricted during each plosive or sibilant sound in such cases.

These mechanical limitations of articulation in cleft palate lead to secondary modifications of behaviour. Linguistic ability is retarded through general limitation of speech learning. Emotional reactions to the handicap may complicate the clinical picture, and hence a vicious circle is established, which in turn impedes the sufferer's general intellectual and special linguistic development.

Other coincidental disorders complicate the pattern of cleft-palate speech. Many cleft-palate patients also suffer from middle-ear infection, and the resulting hearing loss may add the component of audiogenic dyslalia. In other cases, the structural malformation may be complicated by intellectual disability. Coincidental genetic factors may aggravate the speech problem when the syndrome of familial (neurally inherited) language disability is superimposed. In such cases, the mechanical speech disorder of rhinoglossia becomes complicated by the additional signs of delayed speech development, articulatory dyspraxia, dysgrammatism, and reading and writing disability. This combination is evident in some cases following the successful surgical correction of the palatal deficiency. Although the nasality is promptly alleviated in such cases, the various speech disorders from language disability may persist, since they have nothing directly to do with the previous cleft palate.

Children suffering from cleft lip wait for an examination at the Nanjing Drum Tower Hospital on November 8, 2007, in Nanjing, China. China Photos/Getty Images

Management of cleft palate is the task of a well-coordinated team. The plastic surgeon closes the palatal deficiency, the psychologist analyzes the intellectual endowment, the speech pathologist corrects the various components of disordered speech, the audiologist determines coincidental hearing loss, and the otolaryngologist cares for the health of nose and ears. Tonsils and adenoids may be diseased, leading to the frequent complication of middle-ear infection with hearing loss. This condition may require removal of tonsils and adenoids to preserve hearing. A dilemma is then created. Removal of tonsils and adenoids is generally contra-indicated in cases of deficient palatal closure because this operation increases the degree of open nasality. The child's welfare then should be carefully considered in order to avoid any harm.

When surgical repair is not feasible, the palatal defect may be covered by a special prosthetic plate (obturator) similar to false dental appliances. This technique has been known for many centuries, and various models of obturators have been constructed in the course of time. Cleft-palate care therefore includes the services of a prosthodontist (who makes false teeth) for the optimal construction of such appliances. If worn by children, obturators should be regularly altered to maintain continuous fit as the patient grows.

Well-organized centres for the management of cleft palate are able to offer excellent care so that the speech impediment can be ideally or almost completely corrected in many cases. The problem of cleft palate thus demonstrates once more that human speech requires complex detailed study of its normal functions and manifold approaches for the correction of its imperfections.

TREATMENT AND REHABILITATION

The selection of methods in the medical treatment or educational rehabilitation of communication disorders depends primarily on the underlying basis for the disturbance. Any case of chronic hoarseness should be evaluated first by a laryngologist to establish a precise diagnosis. This is particularly important in the older age groups in which an incipient laryngeal cancer is often overlooked because the patient does not pay attention to his or her deteriorating voice. The prognosis of all cancers becomes rapidly poorer the longer the disease remains unrecognized. As soon as disease of the larynx is excluded as a cause of the vocal complaint, vocal rehabilitation by a competent speech pathologist should be considered.

Malformations, diseases, or injuries of the peripheral speech mechanism are treated by appropriate specialists. The plastic surgeon repairs a cleft of the palate, and the neurologist and internist treat the stroke patient until he or she has recovered sufficiently to be referred for re-education of language abilities. The pediatrician treats the child with intellectual disability, while the geneticist counsels the family regarding the possible inheritance of the disorder and its future avoidance. Deafness or severe hearing loss in early childhood is a typical cause for severe delay of language development and should be promptly recognized through appropriate examination by the ear surgeon (otologist) and hearing specialist (audiologist). Cases of childhood autism (withdrawal, severe eccentricities) or early schizophrenia are now being recognized with increasing frequency by speech pathologists, child psychiatrists, pediatricians, and clinical psychologists. This multitude of various professional interests in the recognition and rehabilitation of such exceptional children is well served by the coordination of these efforts in the modern team approach. But again, the largest group of disorders of voice and speech has causes other than these grossly organic lesions. They belong within the province of speech rehabilitation by experts in speech pathology and other functional practitioners.

DEVELOPMENT OF SPEECH CORRECTION

That humankind has been troubled by speech afflictions since the beginning of recorded history can be gleaned from numerous remarks in the books of the Bible. Further, many scientific and medical writers from the time of antiquity to the Middle Ages reported observations of speech and voice disorders. The recommended remedies merely reflected the inadequacies of the philosophical or empirical notions of their times. Scientifically oriented speech pathology originated in Germany during the latter part of the 19th century, following closely the development of otolaryngology. Three names stand out in this respect: Carl Ludwig Merkel (*Anthropophonik*; 1857), Adolph Kussmaul (*The Disorders of Speech*; 1877), and Hermann Gutzmann, Sr., who became the first professor of speech pathology at the University of Berlin Medical School around 1900.

During the same time, the new science of experimental phonetics was developed by Jean-Pierre Rousselot in Paris, who promptly recognized the great contributions that experimental phonetics could make to the study of normal and disturbed speech. This close collaboration of medical speech pathology with experimental phonetics has remained typical for the European continent where speech correction is customarily carried out under the direction of physicians in the ear, nose, and throat departments of the university hospitals. The designation of speech and voice pathology as logopedics and phoniatrics with its medical orientation subsequently reached many other civilized nations, notably in Japan and on the South American continent. The national organizations in most of these areas are now represented in the International Association of Logopedics and Phoniatrics, which was founded in Vienna in 1924.

The evolution of speech correction in the Anglo-Saxon countries followed a different trend. Although the United Kingdom has had a long tradition in general and experimental phonetics, its College of Speech Therapists was organized as an examining and supervisory body in 1945. Similar organizations followed in other areas of the British Commonwealth.

American speech pathology elected a different way. The American Speech-Language-Hearing Association (ASHA), founded in 1925 in New York City as the American Academy of Speech Correction, became the organizing, examining, and supervisory body for a rapidly growing membership, which surpassed 130,000 by 2008. Many colleges and universities in the United States are accredited by ASHA and offer degrees in speech pathology and audiology, some including work at the doctoral level. The large majority of ASHA members work as speech clinicians. A smaller number with master's degrees and a still smaller number with doctoral degrees staff clinics that deal with communication disorders and that are usually affiliated with hospitals, colleges, universities, and occasionally with civic organizations.

Russian speech correction originally followed the developments of European logopedics and phoniatrics. One facet of early speech pathology research in Russia was its emphasis on Pavlovian theory (conditioning and retraining) and intensive use of neuropsychiatric methods, including pharmacology, sleep therapy, and other intensive treatment programs during hospitalization. Similar trends operated in the eastern European countries, such as in the Czech Republic, where the first independent medical department of logopedics and phoniatrics was organized at the Faculty of Medicine of Charles University in Prague.

SPEECH SYNTHESIS

Speech synthesis is the generation of speech by artificial means, usually by computer. Production of sound to simulate human speech is referred to as low-level synthesis. High-level synthesis deals with the conversion of written text or symbols into an abstract representation of the desired acoustic signal, suitable for driving a low-level synthesis system. Among other applications, this technology provides speaking aid to the speech-impaired and reading aid to the sight-impaired.

PSEUDOLARYNGEAL SPEECH

Pseudolaryngeal speech is mechanical or esophageal speech that is taught by therapists to persons who have had the larynx, or voice box, surgically removed (laryngectomy). The operation is necessary when cancerous growths are present on or near the larynx. After surgery, patients learn to swallow air into the esophagus and belch it out in a controlled manner. The tissues of the gullet act on the ejected air resulting in sound that is altered by oral–nasal structures to produce recognizable speech sounds. Former laryngectomy patients often work with newly diagnosed laryngeal cancer patients before and after surgery to demonstrate that it is possible to learn how to speak again. As a result of this technique, many former laryngeal cancer patients have been able to return to their former occupations and professions.

CHAPTER 6

Disorders of the Nose and Throat and Approaches to Ear, Nose, and Throat Evaluation

Disorders of the nose and throat can affect one's ability to smell, taste, swallow, or even breathe. These conditions arise from a diverse array of causes and are unique in their manifestation. In the case of cleft palate, for example, most instances appear to arise from a combination of genetic and environmental factors, and the disorder is apparent at birth. Laryngeal cancer is also associated with genetic and environmental causes, particularly smoking. However, it generally occurs in adults, and its early detection and treatment are particularly problematic for physicians.

Given the diverse etiology and presentation of disorders of the ear, nose, and throat, approaches to diagnosis and treatment vary greatly. The branch of medicine concerned with the diagnosis, treatment, and evaluation of ear, nose, and throat diseases and disorders is known as otolaryngology. Otolaryngologists are commonly referred to as ear, nose, and throat, or ENT, doctors.

NOTABLE DISEASES AND DISORDERS OF THE NOSE AND THROAT

There are several diseases and disorders of the nose and throat that are notable for reasons of prevalence, severity, or medical or research significance. Perhaps the most common condition of the nose, one experienced by people throughout the world, is nosebleed, which can be caused by any of a number of factors. Most nosebleeds are benign and temporary. Other disorders of the nose, however, can have far more serious consequences for the affected individual's overall health. Included among such disorders are cleft palate, laryngeal cancer, and oral cancer.

LARYNGEAL CANCER

Laryngeal cancer is a malignant tumour of the larynx. There are two types of tumours found on the larynx that can be malignant. One is called a carcinoma, and the other, called a papilloma, often is benign but occasionally becomes malignant.

The papilloma is the most common tumour of the larynx. It is a small warty growth that attaches to the vocal cords or at the joints between the cartilage plates. It is most frequent in singers, announcers, and people who use their voices strenuously and often. In adults it may form many polyps (lumps of tissue) that can plug the larynx. After removal it may reappear. A similar condition may occur in children, except that when they reach puberty the growths usually disappear spontaneously.

Carcinoma of the larynx occurs more often in males. It frequently arises from chronic irritation, overuse of the voice, or alcohol and tobacco abuse. There are two types, called, respectively, intrinsic and extrinsic. The intrinsic form attacks the vocal cords. The tumour originates from the lining of the larynx. It often remains confined to the larynx, and the patient has a good chance of recovery when the tumour is removed. The extrinsic form grows in the area above the vocal cords and folds and may extend to the epiglottis (a flap of cartilage above the larynx) or the pharynx. It usually invades the surrounding tissue and can spread by way of the lymphatic vessels.

Carcinoma begins as a small hard patch or papillary tumour. There may be extensive destruction, ulcers, and abscesses. Laryngeal cancer is a relatively common disease that can be treated in the early stages. Unfortunately, 8 to 10 months may elapse before the first symptoms of hoarseness appear and a diagnosis is made.

Nasal Polyp

A nasal polyp is a lump of tissue that protrudes into the nasal cavity and sometimes obstructs it. Polyps can form as the result of allergic conditions or of inflammation and infection. Allergic polyps are usually bright red because of their extensive network of blood vessels. These polyps are most common along the side and upper walls of the nose. Sometimes they arise in the sinus cavities and emerge into the nasal cavity. They may be treated with drugs (by spray or injection) or excised surgically, but usually they recur until the allergic source is eliminated. Inflammatory polyps result from infections and from injuries to the nose. They do not recur after removal. These polyps contain less fluid than allergic polyps do, but there is an abundance of white blood cells. Polyps can also sometimes arise from closely associated blood vessels that expand as a result of previous injuries to the nose or of high blood pressure.

Nosebleed

Nosebleed, also called epistaxis, is defined simply as an attack of bleeding from the nose. It is a common and usually unimportant disorder but may also result from local conditions of inflammation, small ulcers or polypoid growths, or severe injuries to the skull. Vascular disease,

American tennis player Pete Sampras gets treatment from a doctor for a nose-bleed during the Wimbledon Championships in 1997. Jacques Demarthon/ AFP/Getty Images

such as high blood pressure, may provoke it, and diseases such as scurvy and hemophilia also may be responsible. Usually it is easily controlled by rest and application of cold and pressure. On occasion it may require expert care.

ORAL AND OROPHARYNGEAL CANCER

Oral cancer is a disease characterized by the growth of cancerous cells in the mouth, including the lips. Oral cancer is often associated with cancers of the cavity located behind the tonsils and the back of the throat (oropharyngeal cancer). Most cases originate from the flattened cells that make up the lining of the oral cavity (squamous cell carcinomas). Oral cancers can spread into the jaw and may occur simultaneously with cancers of the larynx, esophagus, or lungs.

Causes and Symptoms

Several factors have been identified that increase the risk of developing oral cancer. Tobacco and alcohol use are the leading factors, with each increasing the risk sixfold. Tobacco use includes cigarettes, cigars, pipes, and chewing tobacco. Oral cancer affects men at twice the rate of women, probably because men have generally been more likely to use tobacco and alcohol. Vitamin A deficiency is also a risk factor, and some strains of human papillomavirus can infect the mouth and may increase risk of oral cancer. Exposure to ultraviolet radiation from the sun is responsible for some cancers of the lips.

Symptoms of oral cancer vary depending on the location of the cancer. The most common symptom is a mouth sore that does not heal. Some early visual signs include white or red patches in the mouth. White patches (leukoplakia) progress to cancer in about 5 percent of cases. The red patches (erythroplakia) bleed easily, and roughly half of them become cancerous. Other symptoms of oral or oropharyngeal cancer include lumps or swelling in the cheek, neck, or jaw, difficulty swallowing or moving the tongue or jaw, and pain in the jaw or teeth. Virtually any type of continuing mouth pain may indicate oral cancer and should be investigated by a physician.

Diagnosis

Once cancer is suspected, a thorough examination is conducted to determine its type and stage. Suspected tumours are analyzed by biopsy, and the mouth, pharynx, and larynx are examined visually with small mirrors or a laryngoscope—a flexible tube that contains a light and lens at the end. In some cases a more extensive examination of the head and neck may be conducted under general anesthesia. Several imaging methods may also be used, such as chest and head X rays, computed tomography (CT) scans, or magnetic resonance imaging (MRI). A swallowed dose of barium may be required before administering X rays in order to provide better image contrast.

Once oral cancer has been diagnosed, its stage is determined to indicate how far the cancer has progressed. Stage 0 oropharyngeal cancer is confined to the epithelial cells that line the oral cavity or pharynx and is sometimes called carcinoma in situ. Stage I and II cancers are less than 2 cm (about ¾ of an inch) and between 2 and 4 cm, respectively, and have not spread to nearby lymph nodes. Stage III tumours are either larger than 4 cm or are smaller cancers that have spread to one lymph node on the same side of the neck as the tumour. Stage IV tumours have spread to other regions of the neck, the lymph nodes, or other organs in the body. Survival is considerably higher when the cancer is detected early but very low once the cancer has spread to distant organs.

Treatment and Prevention

Like most cancers, oral and oropharyngeal cancers can be treated with surgery, radiation, or chemotherapy. Surgery is often the first mode of treatment. In order to minimize tissue loss, superficial cancers of the lip may be shaved off a layer at a time until no cancer is detected. Small early-stage tumours can be removed along with some surrounding tissue with minimal side effects. If the cancer has spread into the surrounding bone, part or all of the jaw may have to be removed (mandible

Dental hygiene student Audrey Rayniak gives an oral cancer screening to a patient at a free dental clinic on September 11, 2009, in Brighton, Colorado. John Moore/Getty Images

resection) or a maxillectomy performed to remove the hard palate. Both of these procedures require subsequent reconstructive surgery. If the cancer has spread into the lymph nodes of the neck, these nodes will also be removed.

Oral and oropharyngeal cancers may be treated with radiation, using either external beams or surgically implanted radioactive pellets. For oral cancer, external radiation is the most common approach. Radiation is usually employed in conjunction with surgery to destroy small amounts of remaining cancerous tissue.

Oral cancer is almost completely preventable if the key risk factors of smoking and alcohol consumption are avoided. A healthy diet containing sufficient vitamin A is also recommended. Regular dental examinations may detect oral cancer early. Dentures should be removed and cleaned at night to avoid trapping cancer-causing agents against the gums.

SINUS DISORDERS

The most common disorder affecting the paranasal sinuses is infection, a condition that is known as sinusitis. Polyps, consisting of swollen nasal lining, may grow from both the maxillary and ethmoidal sinuses and cause nasal obstruction. They occur most commonly as a result of nasal allergy and require surgical removal. Cancers affecting the paranasal sinuses are rare, especially in the sphenoidal and frontal area. They occur most commonly among the Bantu of South Africa, where they are related to the long-term use of a homemade snuff that is carcinogenic. Certain woodworkers in the furniture industry also have been found to have a greatly increased incidence of nasal sinus cancer.

APPROACHES TO EAR, NOSE, AND THROAT EVALUATION

To assess whether the ear, nose, and throat are structurally normal and functioning properly, ENT doctors rely on different methods of evaluation. Hearing, for example, can be assessed through a range of approaches, from basic tuning-fork tests to sophisticated testing with an audiometer. Although the science behind ear, nose, and throat evaluation has its origins in the 19th century, and therefore has a relatively brief history as a formal area of medical science, otolaryngology and related disciplines experienced tremendous advances in the 20th and early 21st centuries.

OTOLARYNGOLOGY

Otolaryngology (or otorhinolaryngology) is a medical specialty concerned with the diagnosis and treatment of diseases of the ear, nose, and throat. Traditionally, treatment of the ear was associated with that of the eye in medical practice. With the development of laryngology in the late 19th century, the connection between the ear and throat became known, and otologists became associated with laryngologists.

The study of ear diseases did not develop a clearly scientific basis until the first half of the 19th century, when Jean-Marc-Gaspard Itard and Prosper Ménière made ear physiology and disease a matter of systematic investigation. The scientific basis of the specialty was first formulated by William R. Wilde of Dublin, who in 1853 published *Practical Observations on Aural Surgery, and the Nature and Treatment of Diseases of the Ear.* Further advances were made with the development of the otoscope, an instrument that enabled visual examination of the tympanic membrane (eardrum).

The investigation of the larynx and its diseases, meanwhile, was aided by a device that was invented in 1855 by Manuel García, a Spanish singing teacher. This instrument, the laryngoscope, was adopted by Ludwig Türck and Jan Czermak, who undertook detailed studies of the pathology of the larynx. Czermak also turned the laryngoscope's mirror upward to investigate the physiology of the nasopharyngeal cavity, thereby establishing an essential link between laryngology and rhinology. One of Czermak's assistants, Friedrich Voltolini, improved laryngoscopic illumination and also adapted the instrument for use with the otoscope.

In 1921 Carl Nylen pioneered in the use of a highpowered binocular microscope to perform ear surgery; the operating microscope opened the way to several new corrective procedures on the delicate structures of the ear. Another important 20th-century achievement was the development in the 1930s of the electric audiometer, an instrument used to measure hearing acuity.

NASOPHARYNGOLARYNGOSCOPY

Nasopharyngolaryngoscopy is a diagnostic medical procedure that uses a flexible fibre-optic endoscope to visualize the structures inside the nasal passages, including the sinus openings, the larynx, and the vocal cords. The type of endoscope used for this procedure is called a nasopharyngolaryngoscope. This instrument enables a more thorough examination to be performed than is possible with indirect visualization with a mirror.

HEARING TESTS AND REHABILITATION

Before the development of electroacoustic equipment for generating and measuring sound, the available tests of hearing gave approximate answers at best. A person's hearing could be specified in terms of the ability to distinguish the ticking of a watch or the clicking of coins or the distance at which conversational speech or a whispered voice could be understood. The examiner also might note the length of time the person could hear the gradually diminishing note of a tuning fork, comparing the performance with his or her own.

Tuning-Fork Tests

A qualitative assessment of hearing loss can be carried out with a tuning fork. These tests exploit the ability of sound to be conducted through the bones of the skull. In the Rinne test the sounding tuning fork is placed on the mastoid process, and the person being tested is asked to report when it is no longer heard. The examiner then removes the fork immediately and holds the prongs close to the open ear canal. The normal ear continues to hear it for about 45 seconds, and this "positive" result occurs also with incomplete sensorineural impairment of hearing. When the result is "negative" and the fork is heard longer by bone conduction than by air conduction, a conductive type of deafness is present. In the Schwabach test the presence of a sensorineural impairment is indicated when the individual being tested cannot hear the bone-conducted sound as long as the examiner with normal hearing can. The individual with a conductive hearing loss, however, can hear the fork for a longer period of time than the examiner because the conductive lesion excludes the extraneous airborne masking noise of the surroundings. A bone-conduction audiometer would give a similar result.

For the Weber test, the fork is simply placed on the person's forehead, and the examiner asks in which ear the person hears it. If a sensorineural lesion is present in one ear, the person will localize the sound in the opposite, or "better," ear. If a conductive defect is present, the person will localize it in the "worse" ear—i.e., the one that is protected from interference by extraneous sounds. This simple test has been a valuable aid in the diagnosis of otosclerosis for many years.

Audiometry

With the introduction of the electric audiometer in the 1930s, it became possible to measure an individual's hearing threshold for a series of pure tones ranging from a lower frequency of 125 hertz to an upper frequency of 8,000 or 10,000 hertz. This span includes the three octaves between 500 and 4,000 hertz that are most important for speech.

The audiometer consists of an oscillator or signal generator, an amplifier, a device called an attenuator, which controls and specifies the intensity of tones produced, and an earphone or loudspeaker. The intensity range is usually 100 decibels in steps of 5 decibels. The "zero dB" level represents normal hearing for young adults under favourable, noise-free laboratory conditions. It was established in 1964 as an international standard.

In pure-tone audiometry each ear is tested separately, while the other is shielded against sound. The person being tested wears an earphone or sits in front of a loudspeaker in a quiet test chamber, with instructions to give a hand signal whenever a brief tone is sounded. The audiologist proceeds to determine the lowest intensity for each frequency at which the person reports being just able to hear the tone 50 percent of the time. For example, one who hears the tone of 4,000 hertz only half the time at the 40-decibel setting has a 40-decibel hearing level for that frequency—i.e., a threshold 40 decibels above the normal threshold. A graph showing the hearing level for each ear by octaves and half octaves across the frequency range of 125 to 8,000 hertz is called an audiogram. The shape of the audiogram for an individual who is hard-of-hearing can provide the otologist or audiologist with important information for determining the nature and cause of the hearing defect. (The audiologist is primarily concerned with measuring the degree of hearing impairment, whereas the otologist diagnoses and treats defects and diseases of the ear by medical or surgical means.)

A calibrated bone-conduction vibrator usually is furnished with the audiometer so that hearing by bone conduction also can be measured. When an individual has otosclerosis or another conductive defect of the middle ear, there may be a sizable difference between the air-conduction and bone-conduction audiograms, the so-called air-bone gap. This difference is a measure of the loss in transmission across the middle ear and indicates the maximum improvement that may be obtained through successful corrective surgery. When the defect is confined to the organ of Corti, the bone-conduction audiogram shows the same degree of loss as the air-conduction audiogram. In such cases of sensorineural impairment, surgery is seldom capable of improving hearing, but a hearing aid may be helpful.

Although faint sounds may not be heard at all by the ear with a sensorineural impairment, more intense sounds may be as loud as they are to a healthy ear. This rapid increase in loudness above the threshold level is called recruitment. When the opposite ear has normal hearing, recruitment can be measured by the alternate binaural loudness balance test. The subject is asked to set the controls so that the loudness of the tone heard in the defective ear matches that of the tone heard in the normal ear. By repeating the comparison at several intensity levels, the presence or absence of recruitment can be demonstrated. When recruitment is excessive, the range of useful hearing between the threshold and the level at which loudness becomes uncomfortable or intolerable may be narrow, so that the amplification provided by a hearing aid is of limited value to the subject.

Although hearing thresholds for pure tones give some indication of the person's ability to hear speech, direct measurement of this ability is also important. Two types of tests are used most often. In one test the speech reception threshold is measured by presenting words of spondee pattern—i.e., words containing two syllables of equal emphasis, as in "railway" or "football"—at various intensity levels until the level is found at which the person can just hear and repeat half the words correctly. This level usually corresponds closely to the average of the person's thresholds for frequencies of 500, 1,000, and 2,000 hertz. A more important measure of socially useful hearing is the discrimination score. For this test a list of selected monosyllabic words is presented at a comfortable intensity level, and the subject is scored in terms of the percentage of words heard correctly. This test is helpful in evaluating certain forms of hearing impairment in which the sounds may be audible but words remain unintelligible. Such tests usually are carried out in a quiet, sound-treated room that excludes extraneous noise. These tests may give an overly optimistic impression of the ability of the individual with a sensorineural impairment to understand speech in ordinary noisy surroundings. For this reason speech tests are best carried out against a standardized noise background as well as in the quiet. A person with a conductive defect may be less disturbed by the noisy environment than a healthy subject. More elaborate tests, which often involve speech or sound localization, are available for evaluating hearing when central defects of the auditory system are suspected as a result of aging, disease, or injury. Their interpretation may be difficult, however, and the diagnostic information they furnish may be unclear.

When the hearing of infants or others who are unable to cooperate in standard audiometric tests must be measured, their thresholds for pure tones can be established by electrophysiological means. One type of test is the electrocochleogram (ECoG). Electric potentials representing impulses in the cochlear nerve are recorded from the outer surface of the cochlea by means of a fine, insulated needle electrode inserted through the tympanic membrane to make contact with the promontory of the basal turn. This test provides a direct sampling of cochlear function.

A noninvasive, painless, and more frequently used test is brain-stem-evoked response audiometry (BERA). In this test electrodes are pasted to the skin (one placed behind the ear) and are used to record the neural responses to brief tones. The minute potentials evoked by a train of brief sound stimuli are suitably amplified and averaged by a small computer to cancel out background activity, such as potentials from muscles or the cerebral cortex. The typical recording shows a series of five or six waves that represent the responses of successive neural centres of the auditory pathway of the brainstem and provide information about the strength and timing of their activity.

A simple and objective means of testing hearing at the level of the cochlea and brainstem is supplied by impedance audiometry. Two small tubes are sealed into the external canal. Through one tube sound from a small loudspeaker is injected into the canal. The portion that is reflected from the tympanic membrane is picked up by the other tube and led to a microphone, amplifier, and recorder. When a sudden, moderately intense sound is applied to the opposite ear, the stapedius muscle contracts, the impedance is increased, and the recorder shows a slight excursion as more sound is reflected. This test can provide information not only about the condition of the cochlea and the auditory pathways of the medulla but also about the facial nerve that innervates the stapedius muscle. However, it does not give an actual measurement of the acoustic impedance of the ear, representing the state of the ossicular chain and the mobility of the tympanic membrane. This information can be obtained by means of the acoustic bridge—a device that enables the examiner to listen simultaneously to a sound reflected from the tympanic membrane of the subject and a sound of equal intensity reflected in an artificial cavity, with the volume being adjusted to equal that of the external canal of the ear being tested. When the two sounds are matched by varying the acoustic impedance of the cavity, the impedance of the ear is equal to that of the cavity, which can be read directly from the scale of the instrument. Conductive defects of the middle ear, including disarticulation (separation) of the ossicular chain and immobility of the malleus or stapes, can be recognized by the characteristic changes they cause in the impedance of the ear as revealed by tympanometry. This test procedure consists in raising and lowering the air pressure in the middle ear to alter the stiffness in the tympanic membrane while measuring the changes in its compliance in terms of the amount of sound reflected from it. Profound sensorineural deafness can occur as a result of viral and other infection, including mumps, measles, and meningitis. Rubella in the mother during pregnancy can cause severe damage to the organ of Corti, resulting in profound hearing impairment in the child. Cochlear abnormalities may be present also as a result of genetic defects. The electrophysiological hearing tests described above—BERA and ECoG—make it possible to detect such loss in infants. In all such cases of deafness in young children it is essential that the condition be recognized as early as possible so that appropriate counseling in matters of care and education may be obtained. As an important aid in learning to speak, surgical implantation of an electronic cochlear prosthesis should be considered before the child reaches school age. These devices, while controversial within the deaf community, are proving effective in restoring a significant degree of hearing to many young children with congenital deafness.

Rehabilitation of Hearing Impairment

The child born deaf or with a severe hearing impairment cannot acquire speech by the normal process but must attend special classes or a school for the deaf to be taught speech and lipreading. Most of these children have remnants of the sense of hearing that can be utilized in their schooling by the use of aids to amplify sound. The child with a moderate or mild hearing impairment is able to acquire speech independently but a little more slowly than the child with normal hearing, while speech-correction instruction is usually required to improve diction. Cochlear implants can be considered for children and adults with a total absence of hearing or hearing loss so profound that hearing aids are not helpful. Implants make it possible for a deaf child to develop speech and allow a deaf adult to communicate more effectively.

Advances in hearing-aid technology have served to increase the proportion of hearing-impaired individuals who can benefit substantially from amplification. Selection of an appropriate hearing aid for individuals with sensorineural (or nerve-type) hearing loss may be difficult and time-consuming. Research has demonstrated repeatedly, however, that the ability of listeners with sensorineural hearing loss to understand speech at conversational levels often can be enhanced significantly by use of an appropriate hearing aid. For those individuals whose hearing loss causes severe distortion of speech, use of a hearing aid in combination with lipreading may increase the amount of speech the individual can understand through lipreading alone. On the other hand, selection of a hearing aid is often a simpler matter for listeners with hearing loss of the conductive type. Careful selection is necessary to ensure that maximum understanding of speech is obtainable in noisy environments. The hearing-impaired individual should consult with trained professionals such as audiologists, who are trained in evaluating the benefit derived from the use of a hearing aid.

Lipreading, which actually entails attentive observation of the entire facial expression rather than the movements of the lips alone, is used even by persons with normal hearing who, in the presence of background noise, need these visual clues to supplement hearing. As hearing begins to be impaired, lipreading, which might better be termed speechreading, becomes increasingly valuable and important.

The hearing-impaired individual who knows a spoken language can learn lipreading by careful observation of a speaker of that language. Formal instruction in lipreading by a teacher individually or in classes is necessary for those hearing-impaired persons who have not acquired knowledge of a spoken language. The greater the loss of hearing, the more essential lipreading becomes, for which good lighting is essential. The hearing-impaired may also be taught a sign language, such as American Sign Language, as a communications tool.

Speech-correction instruction, needed for the young with serious degrees of impaired hearing, also becomes necessary for the adult who suddenly loses all hearing in both ears. Without the monitoring effect of hearing one's own voice, speech begins to deteriorate and to acquire the flat, toneless quality of the profoundly deaf.

Hearing Aids

A hearing aid is a device that increases the loudness of sounds in the ear of the wearer. The earliest aid was the ear trumpet, characterized by a large mouth at one end for collecting the sound energy from a large area and a gradually tapering tube to a narrow orifice for insertion in the ear.

Modern hearing aids are electronic. Principal components are a microphone that converts sound into a varying electrical current, an amplifier that amplifies this current, and an earphone that converts the amplified current into a sound of greater intensity than the original. Early models were quite large, but when transistors replaced amplifier tubes and smaller magnetic microphones became available in the 1950s, it became possible to build very small hearing aids, some of which were constructed to fit within the frames of eyeglasses and, later, behind the earlobe or within the external ear.

Hearing aids have widely differing characteristics; requirements for suitable aids have been extensively investigated. The two characteristics of a hearing aid that most influence the understanding of speech are the amplification of the various components of speech sounds and the loudness with which the sounds are heard by the wearer. As regards the first characteristic, speech sounds contain many components of different frequencies, which are variously amplified by a hearing aid. The variation of amplification with frequency is called the frequency response of the aid. An aid need amplify sounds only within the range of 400 to 4,000 hertz, although the components of speech cover a much wider range. With regard to the second characteristic—the loudness with which sounds are heard—too loud a sound can be as difficult to understand as one that is too faint. The loudness range over which speech is understood best is wide for some users and narrow for others. Hearing aids with automatic volume control vary the amplification of the aid automatically with variations of the input. A binaural hearing aid consists of two separate aids, one for each ear. Such an arrangement can benefit certain users.

Cochlear Implant

A cochlear implant is an electrical device inserted surgically into the human ear that enables the detection of sound in persons with severe hearing impairment. Cochlear implants are most often used in adults affected by profound sensorineural deafness, although children

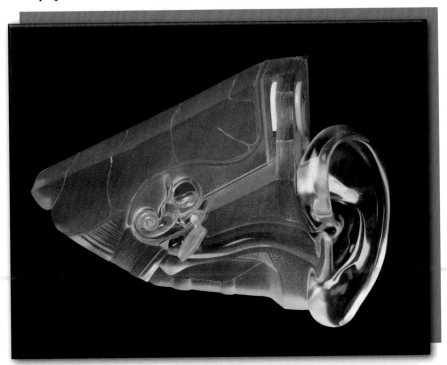

Cochlear implants help profoundly deaf people to hear. A mini-processor creates simple digital versions of sound and sends it to a receiver implanted inside the wearer's head. SSPL via Getty Images

with this form of deafness who do not benefit from external hearing aids may also be candidates for cochlear implantation.

Modern cochlear implants have both external and internal components. External parts include a microphone, the tip of which rests just above the external auditory canal; a sound processor, which organizes sound detected by the microphone; and a transmitter, which consists of an electrical coil held in place by a magnet and conducts information via electromagnetic induction or radio frequency from the processor to a receiver/stimulator that lies beneath the skin. The receiver/stimulator is anchored in the temporal bone and is one of the two primary internal components of the cochlear device, the second being an electrode array that is implanted along the cochlear nerve fibre. The receiver/stimulator converts transmitter signals into electrical impulses, which are relayed along a cable to the electrode array. This mechanism of impulse conduction mimics the normal function of the cochlear nerve by stimulating nerve fibres that lead to the auditory nucleus.

Many patients with cochlear implants experience immediate improvements in hearing, and those who benefit most rapidly tend to be adults who lost their hearing after having already developed extensive language and speech skills. Young children who undergo intense therapy following implantation often make substantial gains in speech recognition and in their ability to discern different types of sound, including loud and soft sounds. Some individuals with cochlear implants eventually can even understand speech without lip reading. However, not all patients benefit to this extent, and a few actually may experience a complete loss of hearing in the affected ear as a result of the implantation procedure or the presence of the implant itself. Other side effects associated with the procedure or the device include infection, numbness around the ear, tinnitus (a constant ringing or buzzing noise in the ears), implant failure, and injury to the facial nerve, which runs through the temporal bone and passes close to the vestibulocochlear nerve. Surgical implantation of a cochlear device requires general anesthesia.

The first successful implantation of electrodes capable of stimulating the auditory nucleus was reported in 1957 by French otolaryngologists André Djourno and Charles Eyriès, who embedded electrodes near the cochlear nerve of a patient who was suffering from a condition known as cholesteatoma (the growth of a cyst in the middle ear that results in hearing loss). Later refinements in cochlear implant technologies led to the development of multichannel electrode arrays, which enable patients to sense different frequencies of complex sounds and to recognize speech patterns. Advances in electrode technologies and device materials have reduced the risk of infection associated with cochlear implants. In addition, reductions in the sizes of external parts have given newer devices a relatively discreet appearance, although in young children the microphone and transmitter are often conspicuous. Despite these vast improvements in cochlear implant technology, however, the long-term effects of the electrodes on the nerves and function of the auditory nucleus remain unknown.

Other Communications Options

The communications strategies that are adopted by an individual affected by hearing loss are influenced by the cause and severity of the hearing impairment and the person's age at its onset. The approaches emphasized in preceding sections have focused mainly on devices, such as cochlear implants, that help deaf persons communicate through spoken language. However, other approaches may be taken as well, one of the most commonly used of which is sign language, a means of communicating through body movements, especially of the hands and arms. Other approaches to facilitating communication for persons with hearing loss include speech correction, lipreading, and technologies such as closed-captioned television.

In sign languages, concepts are expressed with a delicately nuanced combination of coded hand signals reinforced by facial expressions. They may sometimes be augmented by a manual alphabet, used to spell out each letter of a word by either a one-hand or two-hand system. More than 100 different sign languages exist. These sign languages have more in common with one another than with the spoken languages of their country of origin, since their signs represent concepts and not words. Each sign language has its own complex syntax and grammar and is a complete, independent language. The sign language native to the United States is American Sign Language. As with spoken language, a person's ability to learn a sign language is greatly increased if he or she is exposed to it from a very early age.

Deafness interferes with a person's ability to speak as well as to listen to spoken language. Hearing helps a person regulate his or her speech by providing constant feedback about the tone and volume of the voice and the accuracy of how sounds are expressed. People who become completely deaf as adults or older children may need speech-correction instruction in order to continue to speak normally. Children born with severe to total hearing loss cannot learn to speak without special instruction. Those born with mild to moderate hearing loss may acquire speech on their own but at a slower rate than children who are able to hear normally. They also may benefit from speech therapy.

An Iraqi teacher teaches deaf girls sign language in 2006 in Baghdad. Sabah Arar/AFP/Getty Images

Many people with hearing loss use lipreading, or speech reading, to help them understand spoken language. This entails observing the movement of a speaker's lips and face to obtain visual cues to aid in recognizing spoken words. Speech reading may be supplemented by cued speech, a visual system that uses the natural mouth movements of speech along with hand signs in various positions to represent speech sounds.

Technology comes to the aid of the hard of hearing in many ways. Special instrumentation, such as videophones (as with Skype) and devices that use lights or vibrations to signal the ring of a doorbell or alarm clock, can help make everyday life more convenient. Closed-captioned television helps deaf people follow the audio portion of television programs by displaying on the screen a text transcription of the dialogue as it is spoken.

Genetic Testing for Deafness

Gains in understanding the genetic basis of sensory impairments in humans have raised moral and legal questions, in large part because of the possibilities presented for prenatal diagnosis of these impairments and for their early diagnosis and intervention after birth. Issues that must be considered include, for example, whether the option of terminating a pregnancy should be offered to "hearing" parents of a child who will be born deaf or to deaf parents of a child who will be born "hearing." Similarly, mandated newborn screening for profound hearing impairment, with the clear intent to encourage early intervention, has been taken by some members of the deaf community as a threat to the continued existence of the well-established deaf language and culture. Clearly, these issues emerge from differing opinions of what is a disease and what is simply a trait. Such dilemmas over sensory impairment remain but the tip of the iceberg with regard to human genetics. How individuals and societies handled these specific questions will set a precedent for the many similar problems that lie ahead.

CONCLUSION

Although a great deal is known about the anatomy and physiology of the ear, nose, and throat, there remains much to be learned about these tissues. One area of ongoing investigation centres around the timing and sequence of formation of the sensory structures of the ear during embryological development. Using the powerful tools of genetic analysis that are now available, scientists have been able to identify specific genes that play a role in guiding ear development. Equipped with this knowledge, researchers can more effectively study the genes and proteins that are involved in ear function and how and why they become dysfunctional to give rise to disorders such as congenital hearing loss. Such studies may result ultimately in the development of new treatments or disease-prevention strategies.

Similar research on the molecular features of tissues that make up the nose and throat has led to important advances in scientists' understanding of a variety of diseases and disorders. For example, in a condition known as Kallmann syndrome, affected individuals lose their sense of smell (anosmia). Research has revealed that this condition is caused by a mutation in a gene that directs the formation of the olfactory system and the formation of parts of the region of the brain known as the hypothalamus. The genetic defect also results in hypogonadism and deficiency of a substance known as gonadotropin-releasing hormone. A condition known as specific anosmia, in which the affected individual loses the ability to sense a particular odour, also appears to have a genetic basis. Humans have a genetically encoded system of odour recognition consisting of receptors that bind specific odorant molecules that fall within seven classes of so-called primary odours. The complexity of odorants and their interactions with receptors in the olfactory system is reflected in studies of specific anosmia in mice, which have indicated that deficits in the ability to recognize a specific odour may actually entail defects in more than one type of odorant receptor.

Paralleling research on the genetics of disorders ranging from hearing loss to anosmia are investigations of environmental factors that may also contribute to these conditions. The interplay of genetics and the environment is striking in its complexity, and teasing out the contributions of each is expected to remain an important goal in future work.

GLOSSARY

acoustic impedance The ratio of sound-pressure amplitude to volume-velocity amplitude across a given surface in a medium transmitting sound.

anosmia Loss or impairment of the sense of smell.

articulation The act of giving utterance or expression.

auricle An angular or ear-shaped lobe, process, or appendage.

axon A usually long and single nerve-cell process that usually conducts impulses away from the cell body.

basilar Of, relating to, or situated at the base.

cerumen Earwax.

cuticular Of or relating to an outer covering layer.

dyscrasia An abnormal condition of the body and especially the blood.

dysphonia Defective use of the voice.

endolymph The watery fluid in the membranous labyrinth of the ear.

epistaxis Nosebleed.

etiologic Assigning or seeking to assign a cause.

ganglion A mass of nerve tissue containing cell bodies of neurons external to the brain or spinal cord.

gustation The act or sensation of tasting.

innervate To supply with nerves.

kinocilium A motile cilium, especially one that occurs alone at the end of a sensory hair cell of the inner ear among numerous nonmotile stereocilia.

labyrinth A tortuous anatomical structure, especially the inner ear or its bony or membranous part.

larynx The upper part of the windpipe that in humans and most mammals contains the vocal cords.

macula An anatomical structure having the form of a spot differentiated from surrounding tissues.

mastoid process The process of the temporal bone behind the ear that is well developed and of somewhat conical form in adults but inconspicuous in children.

olfaction The act or process of smelling.

ossicular chain A row of small bones or bony structures (as the malleus, incus, or stapes).

perilymph The fluid between the membranous and bony labyrinths of the ear.

petrous Of, relating to, or constituting the exceptionally hard and dense portion of the human temporal bone that contains the internal auditory organs.

proprioceptive Of, relating to, or being stimuli arising within the organism.

saccule A little sac; specifically, the smaller chamber of the membranous labyrinth of the ear.

sensorineural Of, relating to, or involving the aspects of sense perception mediated by nerves.

stapes The innermost ossicle of the middle ear of mammals.

stereocilium A specialized microvillus that superficially resembles a cilium and projects from the surface of certain cells (as the auditory hair cells and the superficial epithelial cells of the epididymis).

striola A faint or minute stria.

superior olivary complex A small gray nucleus situated dorsal to the inferior olive and made up of cells in the auditory path.

transduction The act or process of converting (as energy or a message) into another form.

tympanic membrane A thin membrane that closes externally the cavity of the middle ear and functions in the mechanical reception of sound waves and in their transmission to the site of sensory reception.

utricle The part of the membranous labyrinth of the inner ear into which the semicircular canals open.

vestibule The central cavity of the bony labyrinth of the inner ear or the parts (as the saccule and utricle) of the membranous labyrinth that it contains.

BIBLIOGRAPHY

HEARING, SMELL, AND TASTE

A useful introduction to the study of the human ear and hearing is Teri A. Hamill and Lloyd L. Price, *The Hearing Sciences* (2008). An exploration of the relationship between sound and the brain is Jan Schnupp, Israel Nelken, and Andrew King, *Auditory Neuroscience: Making Sense of Sound* (2011). The physics of sound and the relevance of sound to the human ear, hearing, and sound perception is William J. Mullin et al., *Fundamentals of Sound with Applications to Speech and Hearing* (2003).

A book dealing specifically with the senses of taste and smell is Gary K. Beauchamp and Linda Bartoshuk (eds.), *Tasting and Smelling* (1997). A work providing insight on the perception of taste and flavour in humans is Andrew J. Taylor and Deborah D. Roberts (eds.), *Flavor Perception* (2004).

EAR DISEASES

A well-illustrated text on diseases of the ear and their surgical correction is Aina Julianna Gulya, Lloyd B. Minor, Dennis S. Poe (eds.), *Glasscock-Shambaugh Surgery of the Ear*, 6th ed. (2010). Additional information on diseases and disorders of the ear can be found in Maurice H. Miller and Jerome D. Schein, *Hearing Disorders Handbook* (2008); Barbara R. Schirmer, *Psychological, Social, and Educational Dimensions of Deafness* (2001); and Patrick J. Willems (ed.), *Genetic Hearing Loss* (2004). A useful review in lay language of the problem of deafness and the adverse influence on hearing of excess noise exposure is Karl D. Kryter, *The Handbook of Hearing and the Effects of Noise: Physiology, Psychology, and Public Health* (1994).

COMMUNICATION DISORDERS

An introduction to the human faculty of speech and its relationship with hearing and language is John Anthony Seikel, Douglas W. King, and David G. Drumright, *Anatomy & Physiology for Speech, Language, and Hearing*, 3rd ed. (2005). An overview of disorders of communication is Robert E. Owens, Jr., Dale E. Metz, and Adelaide Haas, *Introduction to Communication Disorders: A Life Span Perspective*, 2nd ed. (2003). The diagnosis and treatment of communication disorders is explored in Rhea Paul and Paul W. Cascella (eds.), *Introduction to Clinical Methods in Communication Disorders*, 2nd ed. (2007); and Dennis C. Tanner, *Exploring the Psychology, Diagnosis, and Treatment of Neurogenic Communication Disorders* (2010).

INDEX

A

acoustic bridge, 155
acoustic impedance, 31, 155
acoustic meatus, 4
acoustic neuroma, 113
actin, 23, 43
acute middle ear infection, 101–103
adaptation, 85, 91
adenoids, 72–75, 131, 134
aero-otitis media, 102–103
aglossia, 130
air conduction, 31–35, 106, 150, 152
air pressure, 11, 69, 102–103, 155
air sinuses, 63–65
alcoholism, 87, 141, 144
allergies, 99, 102–103, 114, 142, 147
American Sign Language (ASL), 157, 162
American Speech-Language-Hearing Association (ASHA), 138
amplification, 158–160
ampullae, 15, 16, 53
anatomy
  brain, 37, 48
  cochlea, 11–12, 17–21
  ear, 2, 3–27
  inner ear, 3, 6, 11–25
  middle ear, 3, 5–11
  nose, 60–67
  outer ear, 3, 4–5
  throat, 67–74
  tongue, 77
angular acceleration, 52, 54–56
animal experiments, 43–44, 49, 50–51, 55–56
ankyloglossia, 129–130
anosmia, 90–91, 165–166
antibiotics, 44, 58, 96–97, 101, 102, 111, 114
antibodies, 75
anvil (incus), 3, 8, 32, 33, 104
apexes, 5, 14, 17, 20, 39, 49, 63
aqueducts, 15–16, 18
arteries, 6, 17, 116
articulation, 71, 119, 123–127, 129–133
ascending auditory pathways, 45–47
ASHA (American Speech-Language-Hearing Association), 138
ASL (American Sign Language), 157, 162
ataxia, 58
audiograms, 152
audiologists, 116, 134, 136, 152, 157
audiometer, 106, 149, 150, 151, 152
audiometry, 129, 151–156
auditory fibres, 5, 10, 14, 16, 20, 24–25, 36–37, 41, 43, 44–45, 46, 47, 49, 54, 160
auditory nucleus, 1, 28, 37, 44, 161
auditory ossicles, 3, 6–8, 30, 32–34
auditory pathways, 44–48, 50
auricle, 3, 4, 31

aversions, taste, 86–87
axons, 24, 41, 45

B

background noise, 51, 153, 157
balance
    equilibrium, 3, 54–57, 99
    inner ear and, 28, 51–54
basilar membrane, 18–19, 20–21,
    29–30, 35–36, 38–42
basilar papilla, 21–25, 54
BERA (brain-stem-evoked
    response audiometry), 154, 155
bitterness, 78, 79, 82–83, 85
bleeding, nasal, 141, 142–144
blood plasma, 11, 20, 26
blood poisoning, 101
blood vessels, 5, 19, 21, 95, 116, 142
Boettcher's cells, 22, 23
boils, 96
bone conduction, 35–36, 106, 128,
    150, 152
bony labyrinth, 11–13, 15, 16, 26
brain, anatomy of, 37, 48
brainstem, 3, 9, 14, 16, 24–25, 28,
    29–30, 38, 45, 47, 53, 154
brain-stem-evoked response
    audiometry (BERA), 154, 155
Broca's area, 37
bundles, hair, 14, 16, 23, 24, 41,
    42–43, 56, 57
buzzing, in the ears, 115–117, 161

C

calyx, 14, 15
canals
    external auditory, 3, 4, 30, 31, 160
    horizontal, 15–16, 57, 58

posterior, 15
    semicircular, 3, 11, 13, 15–16, 52,
        54–55, 58
    superior, 15, 54, 56
cancer, 69, 99–100, 135, 139,
    141–142, 144–147
capillaries, 19–20, 21, 26
carcinomas, 141–142, 144, 145
carotid artery, 6
cartilage, 4, 61, 95–96
cauliflower ear, 95
cavities
    cranial, 6, 16, 18
    ear, 3, 5–6, 9, 100–102
    nasal, 1, 60–63, 65, 67,
        87–88, 142
    oral, 1, 61, 65–67, 76, 144
    sinus, 2, 60, 62, 63–65, 75,
        142, 147
cells
    of Boettcher, 22, 23
    of Claudius, 22, 23
    of Deiters, 22, 23
    epithelial, 20, 26, 74, 145
    hair cells, 14–15, 16, 18, 21–25,
        28, 29, 34, 36, 41–45, 52,
        56–57, 112, 115
    of Hensen, 22, 23, 24, 25
    mesothelial, 21
    pillar, 21–22, 24, 25, 41
    receptor cells, 1, 13, 56, 76–78,
        79, 80, 87–88, 90, 91, 166
central auditory pathways,
    44–48, 50
central nervous system, 29,
    45–46, 50
cerebellum, 28, 47, 52
cerumen, 5, 94, 99, 115, 117
chemical elements, 89
chewing, 9, 65, 130

children, 5, 71, 72, 75, 94, 108, 119,
    126, 127, 128, 135, 141, 156,
    159–160, 162
chorda tympani nerve, 9, 78
chronic middle ear infection,
    103–104
cilia, 11, 14, 16, 56, 60, 62, 63, 64,
    74, 87
Claudius' cells, 22, 23
cleft palate, 132–135, 140
closed-captioned television,
    163–164
cluttering, 123–124
cochlea, 3, 11–12, 17–25, 27, 29–30,
    34–36, 37–41, 44–47, 108–109,
    154–156, 159–161
cochlear duct, 11–12, 18, 19, 27, 42
cochlear implants, 93, 109, 156,
    159–161
cochlear nerve, 17, 25, 29–30, 41,
    44–48, 93, 154, 160
cocktail party effect, 51
colds, 69, 91, 100, 102, 103, 131
College of Speech Therapists, 137
common cold, 69, 91, 100, 102,
    103, 131
communication disorders
    of articulation, 123–127
    prevalence of, 118–119
    of speech, 71, 119–121, 127–135
    treatment of, 135–139
    of voice, 121–123, 135, 137, 141
computed tomography (CT)
    scans, 107, 145
conchae, 4, 31, 62–63
concussion, 111
conduction, 31–36, 99, 106, 128,
    150, 152
congenital deformity, 98
congenital nerve deafness, 108–110

conversion, 2, 36
Corti, Alfonso, 21, 38
cranial cavities, 6, 16, 18
cranial nerves, 3, 9–10, 116
cristae, 13, 16, 53–54, 56
crus, 8, 15, 16
crystals, 15, 57
CT (computed tomography)
    scans, 107, 145
cupula, 16, 53, 54, 55–56
cuticular plate, 14, 23
cysts, 97, 104, 161
Czermak, Jan, 149

D

Darwin's tubercle, 4
dB (decibels), 29, 32–33, 34, 112, 157
deafness, 93, 107–108, 109, 110,
    128–129, 136, 155–156,
    159–160, 162, 164
decibels (dB), 29, 32–33, 34, 112, 157
deformities, 98–100
Deiters' cells, 22, 23
dendrites, 62
descending auditory pathways,
    47–48
diagnoses, 5, 97, 106–107, 114,
    140, 145, 148, 151, 164
diseases
    diagnoses of, 5, 97, 106–107,
        114, 140, 145, 148, 151, 164
    of inner ear, 104–105, 107–110,
        113–114
    of middle ear, 100–107, 155
    of outer ear, 94–98
    prevention of, 93–94, 127,
        146–147
    of the throat, 69, 141–142,
        144–147

disorders
  of articulation, 123–127
  diagnoses, 5, 97, 106–107, 114,
    140, 145, 148, 151, 164
  of the ear, 93, 94–110, 113–117
  of the nose, 140–141, 142–144
  of speech, 71, 119–121, 123–135
  of the throat, 140–141
  treatment of, 96, 114, 117,
    126–127, 131, 135–139, 140,
    146–147, 148, 156–164
  of the voice, 121–123, 135,
    137, 141
distal process, 20, 24
dizziness, 38, 57–59, 104, 108,
  114, 116
Djourno, André, 161
drainage, 2, 11, 60, 75, 96,
  103–104
drugs, 43–44, 111, 116, 117,
  126, 142
dynamic equilibrium, 54–56
dyscrasia, 121
dysglossic disorders, 129–135
dyslalias, 124, 127–128, 133
dysphemia, 124–127
dysphonia, 121–123

E

ear
  anatomy, 2, 3–27
  auditory ossicles, 3, 6–8, 30,
    32–34
  balance and, 28, 51–54
  cavities, 3, 5–6, 9, 100–102
  cochlea, 3, 11–12, 17–25, 27,
    29–30, 34–36, 37–41,
    44–47, 108–109, 154–156,
    159–161
  deformities of, 98–100
  diseases of, 94–98, 100–110,
    113–114, 155
  fluids in, 11, 23, 26–27, 32, 38, 55,
    93, 101–102, 114
  hair cells, 14–15, 16, 18, 21–25,
    28, 29, 34, 36, 41–45, 52,
    56–57, 112, 115
  hearing and, 28, 30, 31–44
  infections, 95–98, 101–104,
    110, 113, 133
  inflammation of, 113–117
  injury to, 25, 35, 50, 57–58, 78,
    95, 110–113
  inner ear, 3, 6, 11–25, 28,
    35–44, 51–54, 104–105,
    107–114
  middle ear, 3, 5–11, 30, 34–35,
    100–107, 155
  nerves, 3, 5, 9–10, 14, 16, 17, 21,
    24–25, 28, 29–30, 36–38,
    41–42, 44–51, 55–56, 93, 99,
    107–109, 110, 113, 114,
    160–161
  organ of Corti, 18–19,
    21–25, 29–30, 36, 38, 41, 115,
    152, 155
  outer ear, 3, 4–5, 28, 30, 31–34,
    94–100
  semicircular canals, 3, 11, 13,
    15–16, 52, 54–55, 58
  surgery on, 36, 97, 99, 114, 117,
    149, 152
  trauma to, 25, 35, 50, 57–58, 78,
    95, 110–113
  tumours in, 113, 116
  tympanic membrane, 3, 5–11,
    29–30, 31–34, 69, 78, 97, 99,
    102–105, 106, 154–155
earache, 69

eardrum (tympanic membrane), 3, 5–11, 29–30, 31–34, 69, 78, 97, 99, 102–105, 106, 154–155

ear, nose, and throat doctors (ENTs), 131, 134, 140, 148, 161

earphones, 151, 158

earwax, 5, 94, 99, 115, 117

eating
food, 62, 65, 67, 68, 69
tongue and, 65

ECoG (electrocochleogram), 154, 155

eczema, 99

efferent systems, 24, 47

electrical impulses, 1, 38, 154, 160

electrochemical impulses, 2–3, 28, 36

electrocochleogram (ECoG), 154, 155

embryological development, 165

endocochlear potential, 42

endolymph, 12, 16, 18, 23, 26–27, 42, 54, 55

endolymphatic hydrops, 114

ENTs (ear, nose, and throat doctors), 131, 134, 140, 148, 161

epiglottis, 68, 69, 141–142

epistaxis, 141, 142–144

epithelial cells, 20, 26, 74, 145

epithelium, 12, 16, 62–63, 87

epitympanum, 6, 8

equilibrium, 3, 54–57, 99

erysipelas, 96–97

erythroplakia, 144–145

esophagus, 67, 68–69, 71, 139

ethmoidal labyrinths, 64

ethmoidal sinuses, 64, 147

etiologic approach, 127

eustachian tube, 2, 6, 10–11, 69, 75, 93, 100, 102, 103

Ewald, J.R., 55

experimental phonetics, 137

experiments, 26, 40, 43–44, 49, 50–51, 54, 55–56

external auditory canal, 3, 4, 30, 31, 160

eyes, 3, 9, 28, 52, 57, 58

Eyriès, Charles, 161

F

facial expressions, 9, 75, 100, 157, 162

facial muscles, 9, 100

facial nerves, 9, 76, 100–101, 104, 155, 161

falling, sense of, 38, 57–59, 104, 108, 114, 116

feedback loops, 24, 47

fenestrae, 6

fibres
auditory (hearing), 5, 10, 14, 16, 20, 24–25, 36–37, 41, 43, 44–45, 46, 47, 49, 54, 160
gustatory (tasting), 10, 78–80
olfactory (smelling), 62, 87–88

filaments, 14, 23

flavour, 1, 83–84

Flourens, Marie-Jean-Pierre, 54

fluids, in the ear, 11, 23, 26–27, 32, 38, 55, 93, 101–102, 114

food
allergies to, 99, 114
choice of, 86–87
eating of, 62, 65, 67, 68, 69
flavour in, 1, 83–84
smell of, 84
taste of, 76, 84, 86–87

footplate, 6, 8, 32, 33–34, 37–38,
106, 107
fossae, 4, 8, 18, 64, 65
fossa incudis, 8
fragrance, 88–89, 90–91
frequencies, 9, 21, 29, 31, 33,
35–36, 38–41, 49, 71, 112, 115,
128, 151–152, 153, 158
frontal sinuses, 63, 65
frostbite, 95
furuncles, 96

G

ganglion, 17, 24, 41, 44–45
García, Manuel, 149
genetic testing, 164
glomeruli, 87
Goltz, Friedrich, 55
gravity, 13, 15, 28, 52, 56, 59
gustation (taste), 1, 10, 75–87
adaptation, 85
affect on food choices, 86–87
aversions, 86–87
bitterness, 78, 79, 82–83, 85
fibres, 10, 78–80
flavour, 1, 83–84
impulses, 79–80
intensity of, 85
nerves, 76, 78–80
physiological basis, 79–80
qualities of, 80–83
saltiness, 78, 79, 81, 85
sensitivity, 78, 79–80, 84–85
sourness, 78, 80, 85
stimuli, 79, 80, 82, 85–86
sweetness, 78, 79, 80, 82, 85, 86
taste buds, 1, 75–78, 80, 83–84
temperature and, 84–85

tongue and, 10, 76–79, 83
umami, 80, 83
Gutzmann, Hermann, Sr., 137

H

habenula perforata, 24, 45
hair bundles, 14, 16, 23, 24, 41,
42–43, 56, 57
hair cells, 14–15, 16, 18, 21–25, 28,
29, 34, 36, 41–45, 52, 56–57,
112, 115
hairs, sensory, 14, 16, 23–24,
41–43, 54
hammer (malleus), 3, 8, 9, 31–32, 33
hard-of-hearing, speech by,
127–129
hard palate, 61, 65–67, 147
head colds, 69, 91, 100, 102, 103, 131
hearing
diseases affecting, 94–98,
100–110, 113–114, 155
fibres, 5, 10, 14, 16, 20, 24–25,
36–37, 41, 43, 44–45, 46, 47,
49, 54, 160
frequencies, 9, 21, 29, 31, 33,
35–36, 38–41, 49, 71, 112, 115,
128, 151–152, 153, 158
hair cells and, 14–15, 16, 18,
21–25, 28, 29, 34, 36, 41–45,
52, 56–57, 112, 115
impairment of, 36, 51, 110, 150,
152, 155, 156–157, 159
impulses, 14, 16, 21, 28, 29–30,
38, 41, 45, 47, 50–51, 56
inner ear and, 28, 35–44
loss of, 93–94, 102, 105,
109–112, 119, 127–128, 136,
150, 156–157, 161–163

middle ear and, 30, 34–35
nerves, 3, 5, 9–10, 14, 16, 17, 21,
    24–25, 28, 29–30, 36–38,
    41–42, 44–51, 55–56, 93, 99,
    107–109, 110, 113, 114,
    160–161
noise, exposure to, 35, 51, 93–94,
    110, 111–113, 153, 157, 161
outer ear and, 28, 30, 31–34
sound waves in, 1, 2–3, 28–29,
    30–32, 36–41, 128
testing of, 35, 36, 106, 148,
    149–156
vibrations and, 18, 21, 28,
    29–30, 32, 33–34, 35–36, 38,
    39, 40–41, 54, 71
hearing aids, 36, 51, 94, 115, 117,
    128, 156–157, 158–159
helicotrema, 17, 37
helix, 4
Helmholtz, Hermann von,
    38–40
hematoma, 95
Hensen's cells, 22, 23, 24, 25
hertz, 29, 31, 33, 36, 112–113, 115,
    151–152, 158
hoarseness, 135, 142
horizontal canals, 15–16, 57, 58
horizontal plane, 14, 50, 56
hydrodynamic concept, 55
hydrostatic concept, 55

I

impedance, 31, 32–33, 154–155
impediments, of speech, 123–127,
    129–135
implants, cochlear, 93, 109, 156,
    159–161

impulses
    electrical, 1, 38, 154, 160
    electrochemical, 2–3, 28, 36
    hearing, 14, 16, 21, 28, 29–30,
        38, 41, 45, 47, 50–51, 56
    nerve, 14, 16, 21, 28, 29–30, 38,
        41, 45, 47, 50–51, 56, 79–80, 87
    proprioceptive, 52, 58
    smell, 87
    taste, 79–80
incus (anvil), 3, 8, 32, 33, 104
infections, 72, 75, 91, 95–98,
    100–102, 103–104, 110, 113,
    133, 142, 147, 161
inflammation, 113–117
injuries
    to the ear, 25, 35, 50, 57–58, 78,
        95, 110–113
    to the throat, 121–122, 130
    to the tongue, 130
inner ear
    anatomy of, 3, 6, 11–25
    balance and, 28, 51–54
    diseases of, 104–105, 107–110,
        113–114
    hearing and, 28, 35–44
    injury to, 110–113
inner sulcus, 22, 25
innervation, 25, 44, 45, 155
intensity
    of odour, 90
    of sound, 9, 29, 34–35, 49, 151
    of taste, 85
internal meatus, 17, 45
International Association of
    Logopedics and
    Phoniatrics, 137
ions, 26–27, 42–43, 80
Itard, Jean-Marc-Gaspard, 148

J

jugular vein, 6, 101

K

Kallmann syndrome, 165
kinocilia, 14, 16, 23, 41, 56
Kussmaul, Adolph, 137

L

labyrinthitis, 113–114
labyrinths, 3, 6, 11–13, 15, 16,
    18, 26, 27, 52, 54, 55–56,
    64, 101, 107–108, 111,
    113–114
  bony labyrinth, 11–13, 15,
    16, 26
  ethmoidal labyrinths, 64
  membranous labyrinth, 11–13,
    16, 18, 26, 27
  vestibular labyrinth, 54
language, 120–121, 127–128,
    129, 133, 136, 157,
    161–163
laryngeal cancer, 141–142
laryngoscope, 145, 149
larynx (voice box), 1, 67, 69–71,
    78, 121–123, 133, 135, 139,
    141–142, 149
leprosy, 97
lesions, 119, 120, 121, 136, 150
leukoplakia, 144–145
linear acceleration, 52, 56–57
lipreading, 108, 156, 157, 163
lisping, 124
lobule, 4
localization, 46, 50, 153

logopedics, 137–138
long process, 7, 8, 9, 21
loss of hearing, 93–94, 102,
    105, 109–112, 119,
    127–128, 136, 150, 156–157,
    161–163
loudness, 28–29, 41, 46, 49,
    50, 119, 152–153,
    158–159
lymph nodes, 145, 147

M

maculae, 13–15, 52, 56–57
magnetic resonance imaging
    (MRI), 113, 145
malleus (hammer), 3, 8, 9,
    31–32, 33
mastoid process, 6, 35, 36, 150
maxillary sinuses, 64, 65
mechanical vibrations, 36,
    37–38, 41–44
medulla, 45–46, 79
membranous labyrinth, 11–13,
    16, 18, 26, 27
Ménière, Prosper, 114, 148
Ménière disease, 59, 113, 114
meningitis, 101, 104, 113, 155
Merkel, Carl Ludwig, 137
mesothelial cells, 21
microvilli, 76
middle ear
  anatomy, 3, 5–11
  diseases of, 100–107, 155
  hearing and, 30, 34–35
  muscles, 8–9, 34–35, 154–155
  nerves, 8–9
modiolus, 17, 19, 20, 41, 45
motion sickness, 58

mouth
  anatomy, 67–74
  chewing, 9, 65, 130
  diseases of, 69, 141–142, 144–147
  disorders of, 140–141
  eating and, 62, 65, 67, 68, 69
  injury to, 121–122, 130
  patches in, 144–145
  pharynx, 10–11, 67–69, 72,
    74–75, 133, 145
  surgery on, 139, 146–147
  swallowing, 9, 11, 60, 62, 67,
    69, 74, 84, 103, 130, 145
  tumours in, 141–142, 145–146
MRI (magnetic resonance
    imaging), 113, 145
mucous membrane, 5, 9, 62, 63,
    65, 69, 71, 100, 102, 103
mucus, 2, 11, 60, 62, 63, 64, 65,
    74, 87
muscles
  facial, 9, 100
  middle ear, 8–9, 34–35, 154–155
  outer ear, 4
  palate, 67
  reflexes and, 9, 34–35, 57
  throat, 67, 69–71, 74
music, 1, 112, 117
myelin, 24, 45
myosin, 43

N

nares, 61
nasal cavities, 1, 60–63, 65, 67,
    87–88, 142
nasal conchae, 4, 31, 62–63
nasality, 130–132
nasal polyps, 142, 147

nasal speech, 130–132
nasopharyngolaryngoscopy, 149
nasopharynx, 6, 62, 131
nerves
  auditory (hearing), 3, 5, 9–10,
    14, 16, 17, 21, 24–25, 28,
    29–30, 36–38, 41–42, 44–51,
    55–56, 93, 99, 107–109, 110,
    113, 114, 160–161
  chorda tympani nerve, 9, 78
  cochlear, 17, 25, 29–30, 41,
    44–48, 93, 154, 160
  cranial, 3, 9–10, 116
  facial, 9, 76, 100–101, 104, 155, 161
  gustatory (tasting), 76, 78–80
  olfactory (smelling), 62, 64, 84,
    87, 88
  sensory, 5, 9, 78–79
  vagus, 76, 78
  vestibular, 14, 16, 44, 55–56,
    107–108, 111, 114
  vestibulocochlear, 3, 14, 17
neurons, 24, 45, 49, 76, 89
neurotransmitters, 24, 43, 48
noise, 35, 51, 93–94, 110, 111–113,
    153, 157, 161
nose
  anatomy, 60–67
  cavities, 1, 60–63, 65, 67,
    87–88, 142
  concha, 4, 31, 62–63
  disorders of, 140–141, 142–144
  infections in, 100, 142, 147
  nerves, 62, 64, 84, 87, 88
  receptor cells, 1, 87–88, 166
  sensitivity to odours, 88–89,
    90–91
  sinuses, 2, 60, 62, 63–65, 75,
    142, 147

nosebleed, 141, 142–144
nostrils, 11, 61, 62, 84, 133
nuclei, 45, 46, 47
nutritional deficiencies, 101,
      115, 144
Nylen, Carl, 149
nystagmus, 57–58

O

obturators, 135
octaves, 151–152
odorants, 88, 89, 90, 91, 166
odours
      adaptation to, 91
      effects on behaviour, 91–92
      intensity of, 90
      qualities of, 88–89
      sensitivity to, 88–89, 90–91
      stimuli, 90
      temperature and, 90
olfaction (smell), 1, 65, 75, 87–92
      fibres, 62, 87–88
      impulses, 87
      nerves, 62, 64, 84, 87, 88
      receptor cells, 1, 87–88, 166
      sensitivity, 88–89, 90–91
      sexual attraction and, 91–92
oral cancer, 144–147
oral cavities, 1, 61, 65–67, 76, 144
organ of Corti, 18–19, 21–25,
      29–30, 36, 38, 41, 115, 152, 155
oropharyngeal cancer, 144–147
osseous spiral lamina, 17–18, 20,
      24, 43
ossicles, 3, 6–8, 30, 32–34
ossicular chain, 3, 6–8, 31, 32–34,
      102, 104–105, 155
ossicular interruption, 104–105

osteoma, 97
ostia, 63
otic capsule, 6, 35
otic vesicle, 53, 99
otitis media, 93, 101–103, 113, 115
otoconia, 15, 52, 57
otolaryngologists (ENTs), 131,
      134, 140, 148–149, 161
otolaryngology, 131, 134, 137, 140,
      148–149, 161
otolith organs, 13, 28
otoneurology, 58, 59
otorhinolaryngology, 148–149
otosclerosis, 34, 36, 93, 105–107,
      115, 151, 152
otoscope, 5, 148, 149
ototoxic drugs, 43–44, 111
outer ear
      anatomy of, 3, 4–5
      deformities of, 98–100
      diseases of, 94–98
      hearing and, 28, 30, 31–34
      muscles of, 4
outer sulcus, 20
oval window, 6, 30, 32, 33–34, 36

P

pain, 5, 29, 78, 88, 89, 96,
      102–103, 145
palate
      hard palate, 61, 65–67, 147
      muscles of, 67
      soft palate, 10, 61–62, 65–67, 132
palatine tonsils, 68, 72
papillae, 76, 78
papillomas, 141
paralysis, 101, 104, 113, 121,
      130–131

paranasal air sinuses, 63–65
paranosmia, 91
pars tensa, 5, 9
patches, in the mouth, 144–145
pathology
    speech, 120–121, 125, 134,
      135–136, 137–138
    voice, 137
perfume, 90, 91
perilymph, 11–12, 16, 17, 18–20,
    26–27, 32, 33, 37, 42
petrous bone, 3, 9
phalangeal plates, 25
pharynx, 10–11, 67–69, 72, 74–75,
    133, 145
phonetics, 137
phoniatrics, 137–138
pillar cells, 21–22, 24, 25, 41
pinna, 3
pitch, 1, 28–29, 31, 40–41, 49,
    71, 106
planes, directional, 14, 15, 50, 56
plasma, 11, 20, 26
polyps, 142, 147
posterior canals, 15
posture, 28, 57
potassium, 26–27, 42–43, 81
presbycusis, 44, 93, 114–115
primary auditory fibres, 45
processes (projecting parts),
    6, 8, 9, 21, 24, 35, 36, 45,
    76, 150
    axons, 24, 41, 45
    crus, 8, 15, 16
    distal process, 20, 24
    long process, 8, 9, 21
    microvilli, 76
    short process, 8
proprioceptive impulses, 52, 58

proteins, 23, 43
pseudolaryngeal speech, 139

R

radiation, 87, 100, 144, 146, 147
receptor cells
    gravity, 13, 56
    odour, 1, 87–88, 166
    taste, 1, 76–78, 79, 80, 90, 91
red patches, in the mouth,
    144–145
reflexes, 9, 34–35, 57, 86, 89
rehabilitation, 135–139, 156–164
Reissner's membrane, 18–19, 26
research, 126, 127, 138, 156, 165
reticular lamina, 22, 24, 25,
    41–42
rhinoglossia, 132–135
rhombohedral crystals, 15
ringing, in the ears, 115–117, 161
Rinne test, 150
rods of Corti, 21–22, 41
round window, 18, 30, 33–34, 35
Rousselot, Jean-Pierre, 137
rubella, 93, 99, 108, 155

S

saccule, 11, 13–14, 38, 56, 57
saltiness, 78, 79, 81, 85
scala media, 18
scala tympani, 17–18, 33, 35,
    38, 42
scala vestibuli, 17, 19, 33, 35,
    37, 42
secretory otitis media, 101–102
semicircular canals, 3, 11, 13,
    15–16, 52, 54–55, 58

semicircular ducts, 11–12, 16, 53
senses
    hearing, 1, 28–51, 93–98,
        100–110, 113–114, 149–156
    smell, 1, 65, 75, 87–92
    taste, 1, 10, 75–87
    touch, 1, 83, 84
sensitivity
    olfactory, 88–89, 90–91
    taste, 78, 79–80, 84–85
sensorineural impairment, 36,
        51, 110, 150, 152, 155,
        156–157, 159
sensory nerves, 5, 9, 78–79
septicemia, 101
septum, 61, 64
sexual attraction, 91–92
short process, 7, 8
sign language, 108, 157, 162
sinuses, 2, 60, 62, 63–65, 75,
        142, 147
skull fracture, 111
Skype, 163
smell, sense of, 1, 65, 75, 87–92
    fibres, 62, 87–88
    impulses, 87
    nerves, 62, 64, 84, 87, 88
    receptor cells, 1, 87–88, 166
    sensitivity, 88–89, 90–91
    sexual attraction and, 91–92
soft palate, 10, 61–62, 65–67, 132
sound
    amplification, 158–160
    conduction, 31–36, 99, 106,
        128, 150, 152
    decibels, 29, 32–33, 34, 112, 157
    frequencies, 9, 21, 29, 31, 33,
        35–36, 38–41, 49, 71, 112, 115,
        128, 151–152, 153, 158

hertz, 29, 31, 33, 36, 112–113, 115,
        151–152, 158
    intensity of, 9, 29, 34–35, 49, 151
    localization, 46, 50, 153
    loudness, 28–29, 41, 46, 49, 50,
        119, 152–153, 158–159
    noise, 35, 51, 93–94, 110,
        111–113, 153, 157, 161
    overexposure to, 111–112
    pitch, 1, 28–29, 31, 40–41, 49,
        71, 106
    processing of (hearing), 1, 2–3,
        9, 28–51, 94, 104–106,
        152–155
    production of (speech), 1, 69,
        71, 118, 119–135, 138–139,
        162–163
    tone, 40–41, 151, 154
    vibrations and, 18, 21, 28,
        29–30, 32, 33–34, 35–36, 38,
        39, 40–41, 54, 71
sound waves, 1, 2–3, 28–29,
        30–32, 36–41, 128
sourness, 78, 80, 85
speech
    cleft palate, 132–135
    disorders, 71, 119–121, 123–135
    by the hard of hearing, 127–129
    impediments, 123–127, 129–135
    language and, 120–121, 127–128,
        129, 133, 136, 157, 161–163
    nasal, 130–132
    pathology, 120–121, 125, 134,
        135–136, 137–138
    production of, 1, 69, 71, 118,
        119–135, 138–139, 162–163
    pseudolaryngeal, 139
    synthesis of, 138–139
    therapy for, 126–127, 162

speech pathologists, 134, 135, 136
speech reading, 163
sphenoidal sinuses, 64–65
spiral ligament, 18–20
spiral limbus, 18–19, 22, 23
spiral prominence, 20
stammering, 119, 120, 124–127
stapedius, 9, 34–35, 154–155
stapes (stirrup), 3, 8, 9, 32,
    33–36, 37–38, 106, 107, 115
static equilibrium, 56–57
stereocilia, 14, 16, 23–24,
    41–43, 54
stimuli
    odour, 90
    sound, 43, 49
    taste, 79, 80, 82, 85–86
stirrup (stapes), 3, 8, 9, 32,
    33–36, 37–38, 106, 107, 115
stirrup fixation, 105, 115
streptomycin, 58, 111
stria, 18–20, 26–27, 42
stria vascularis, 18, 19, 20,
    26–27, 42
striola, 15
stroke, 47, 121, 136
stuttering, 119, 120, 124–127
sucking reflex, 86
superior canals, 15, 54, 56
superior olivary complex, 46, 47
surgery
    ear, 36, 97, 99, 114, 117, 149, 152
    throat, 139, 146–147
    tongue, 130
swallowing, 9, 11, 60, 62, 67, 69,
    74, 84, 103, 130, 145
sweetness, 78, 79, 80, 82, 85, 86
swelling, 75, 95, 96, 97, 145
synthesis, of speech, 138–139

T

tachyphemia, 123–124
taste, 1, 10, 75–87
    adaptation, 85
    aversions, 86–87
    bitterness, 78, 79, 82–83, 85
    effect on food choices,
        86–87
    fibres, 10, 78–80
    flavour, 1, 83–84
    impulses, 79–80
    intensity of, 85
    nerves, 76, 78–80
    physiological basis, 79–80
    qualities of, 80–83
    receptor cells, 1, 76–78, 79, 80,
        90, 91
    saltiness, 78, 79, 81, 85
    sensitivity, 78, 79–80, 84–85
    sourness, 78, 80, 85
    stimuli, 79, 80, 82, 85–86
    sweetness, 78, 79, 80, 82, 85, 86
    taste buds, 1, 75–78, 80,
        83–84
    temperature and, 84–85
    tongue and, 10, 76–79, 83
    umami, 80, 83
taste buds, 1, 75–78, 80, 83–84
tectorial membrane, 19, 23,
    41–42
teeth, 64, 123, 124, 145
temperature
    odours and, 90
    taste and, 84–85
temporal bone, 3, 6, 9, 17, 36, 160
tensor tympani, 8–9, 34
tests, hearing, 35, 36, 106, 148,
    149–156

therapy, 117, 126–127, 162
throat
  anatomy, 67–74
  cavities, 1, 61, 65–67, 76, 144
  chewing, 9, 65, 130
  diseases of, 69, 141–142,
    144–147
  disorders of, 140–141
  infections in, 100
  injury to, 121–122, 130
  larynx (voice box), 1, 67,
    69–71, 78, 121–123, 133, 135,
    139, 141–142, 149
  muscles, 67, 69–71, 74
  nerve supply, 78
  patches in, 144–145
  pharynx, 10–11, 67–69, 72,
    74–75, 133, 145
  surgery on, 139, 146–147
  swallowing, 9, 11, 60, 62, 67,
    69, 74, 84, 103, 130, 145
  trauma to, 121–122, 130
  tumours in, 141–142,
    145–146
  vocal cords, 1, 71, 120, 141
tinnitus, 115–117, 161
tobacco, 141, 144
tone, 40–41, 151, 154
tongue
  anatomy, 77
  articulation, 71, 123, 124,
    129–130
  eating and, 65
  injury to, 130
  lisping and, 124
  loss of, 130
  nerve supply, 78–79
  receptor cells, 1, 76–78, 79, 80,
    90, 91

  speech disorders and, 120, 123,
    124, 129–130, 145
  surgery on, 130
  taste and, 10, 76–79, 83
  tongue-tie, 129–130
tongue-tie, 129–130
tonsillectomy, 72
tonsillitis, 69, 72
tonsils, 68, 72, 75, 134
toothache, 64
trachea (windpipe), 69–71
tragus, 4
transduction, 2–3, 41–44
trauma
  to the ear, 25, 35, 50, 57–58, 78,
    95, 110–113
  to the throat, 121–122, 130
  to the tongue, 130
treatments, 96, 114, 117, 126–127,
    131, 135–139, 140, 146–147, 148
true aglossia, 130
Tullio phenomenon, 38
tumours, 113, 116, 141–142,
    145–146
tuning, 20–21, 49
tuning fork tests, 35, 36, 106,
    148, 150–151
turbinates, 62, 63
Türck, Ludwig, 149
tympanic annulus, 8
tympanic cavity, 5, 6
tympanic membrane (eardrum),
    3, 5–11, 29–30, 31–34, 69, 78,
    97, 99, 102–105, 106,
    154–155
tympanic ramp (scala tympani),
    17–18, 33, 35, 38, 42
tympanometry, 155
tympanum, 6, 10–11

U

umami, 80, 83
umbo, 8, 31
utricle, 11, 13–14, 16, 52–53, 56–57

V

vagus nerve, 76, 78
Valsalva's maneuver, 11
veins, 6, 17, 20, 101
ventral cochlear nucleus, 46
vertical plane, 14, 15
vertigo, 38, 57–59, 104, 108, 114, 116
vesicles, 24–25, 53, 99, 108
vestibular apparatus, 3, 54, 57–58
vestibular labyrinth, 54
vestibular nerve, 14, 16, 44,
    55–56, 107–108, 111, 114
vestibular ramp (scala vestibuli),
    17, 19, 33, 35, 37, 42
vestibular system, 12–16, 51–54,
    57–59
vestibule, 3, 11, 13–16, 17, 62
vestibulocochlear nerve, 3, 14, 17
vibrations, 18, 21, 28, 29–30, 32,
    33–34, 35–36, 38, 39, 41–44,
    54, 71
videophones, 163
viral nerve deafness, 110
vision, 9, 58

vocal cords, 1, 71, 120, 141
voice
    disorders of, 121–123, 135, 137, 141
    hearing of, 106, 115, 128,
        157–158
    hoarseness, 135, 142
    production of, 71, 106, 119–
        120, 121–123
voice box (larynx), 1, 67, 69–71,
    78, 121–123, 133, 135, 139,
    141–142, 149

W

walls, internal ear, 6, 14, 16
waves, sound, 1, 2–3, 28–29,
    30–32, 36–41, 128
Weber test, 150–151
Wernicke's area, 37
white patches, in the mouth,
    144–145
Wilde, William R., 148
windpipe (trachea), 69–71

X

X rays, 107, 145

Y

yawning, 103